Taking a Minute 3.0

Cover artwork: Holly Sitzler
Art direction and design: Holly Sitzler, Jason Anderson, Juliane Collins
Editor: Tammy Zubeck, Iana Walker, Kelly Rae Hardin

First Edition
ISBN 978-1-58588-166-6 Guys 3.0
ISBN 978-1-58588-167-3 Girls 3.0

3520 East Brown Road
Mesa, Arizona 85213

Printed in the United States of America.

Visit www.takingaminute.com

DEDICATION

To my children, I pray and believe that you will learn to know God in a deeper way than even I have known him.

How To

Turn off the noise. Really. Just for a moment can we turn off the radio, the CD, the MP3, the TV, etc…? Life is bigger when everything is so loud. So turn it down, just for a minute. If you want a life that you enjoy, this is a big part, the ability to be away with God and find out what He wants to do. So hang up the phone for a minute, log off the computer, and try week one. You can do this by setting the alarm clock five minutes early and avoiding the snooze dance or whatever. Give this a try, for no other reason than to gain strength on your inside. God's word works, really, and it's bigger than what you have been through or what you are going through. If you put God in your day, than expect Him to be in your day.

What do I do? Read the short devotional first, follow the pages after, and fill out whatever means something to you. You write down your thoughts so that you can evaluate your year as the year happens. You can start this book at any time, but it will last you a year. David wrote down his thoughts to the Lord. They are in the book of Psalms. If you read the Psalms, it reads like a diary where David wrote his most intimate thoughts and prayers. Prayer works.

There are Bible confessions in each week: SAY THEM OUT LOUD. The out loud part is where the power lives. I'm sure God was thinking about creating the world, but nothing happened until He said it out loud!

There is a place for teaching notes. Take this journal and your Bible to church and take some notes. We are accustomed to taking notes in school so that we can be ready for the test. If you want to be ready for the challenges and tests that life bring, you need to take notes. Godliness is more important than your history class, ya know?

Now turn over the next page and set some goals for this year.

What am I going to start this year? I cannot finish something if I don't start.

How can I help my church grow? Before I'm successful I must first build God's kingdom.

What time of the day am I committing to spending time in this devotional? Pick a time you can stick to, and be a person strong commitment!

How can I improve the atmosphere of my home? We can't always change others, but we can change the atmosphere and ourselves.

What would I want my life to look like in 5 years if there were no limits? Finding the infinite means asking the right question!

Now what can I do to get there?

New Year's Resolution

Another year – another brand new year – and another Taking a Minute. What are you going to do this year? Every New Year most people focus on what they are going to quit. Like, I'm finally going to quit eating fast food. Ha. We all get focused on what we need to stop doing. So forget that for a second, and let me ask you.... what are you going to start doing this year? To be a finisher in life you have to first start. If you don't start something new, then next New Year's Day you will be exactly where you are today. So what are you starting? I went to go for a drive the other day, but my car would not carry me anywhere until I started it. Your life will not carry you anywhere until you start it. Put the key, God's Word, into your heart and turn over your life. God has a plan for you. He wants to direct your footsteps, but He cannot direct feet that are standing still. You can't steer a bike unless it's moving. Try starting college, a business, or that book you've been wanting to write. Maybe you're making a decision to find a church that you will join, or find God. Whatever it is, say it out loud, and get going.

GOD MAIL: Write down some thoughts you want to share with God.

GOD REPLY: Did you hear any thoughts that you think might be from God? Exercise your ability to hear Him, and write it down here.

GOD LOVE: Who are you praying for today? Become others minded by praying for others needs. God will meet your needs! Help others win and God will help you win.

GOD THOUGHT: What are you choosing to think about today? We should always choose our thoughts!

CONFESSING GOD'S WORD

TEACHING NOTES:

Speaker ______________________

Date ______________________

Topic ______________________

CONFESSING GOD'S WORD:

Say this out loud every day this week!

James 2:17

In the same way, faith by itself, if it is not accompanied by action, is dead.

How Old is Your Dad?

Sometimes people ask me, "How old is the earth?" And I say, "I don't know." Whoa, wait, Jason, doesn't the Bible say? Well, about 4004 years BC, or roughly 6000 years ago, God created the heavens and the earth. You can figure that out by adding up all the lineages and years that people lived leading up to Christ, right from the Bible. But how old is the earth? It could be a gajillion years old when you date it, because God created things with age. God didn't create Adam as an infant, but created him as an adult. Imagine He creates a little baby, sticks him in the Garden of Eden. Then He's all, "Well, now we need some diapers." Adam was created with age. And God didn't just make a bunch of bird eggs, he made fully grown birds. He didn't create the sun as a brand new star, but created it as a star with age, and the earth as well. Well this may be a lot to think about, but I think it's important for you to recognize that when your science teacher says, "Well, science says the earth is 4 billion years old," then you can be all, yeah, maybe or maybe it's older or younger, 'cause God is God, and He can create it however old or young He likes. And He made me and you in His likeness and image so that you could have a relationship with Him. And your science teacher might be all like, "Yeah, right" or he might be all "Really, do you know God?" And you can be all, "Yeah He's my Father; would you like to meet him?"

GOD MAIL: Write down some thoughts you want to share with God.

GOD REPLY: Did you hear any thoughts that you think might be from God? Exercise your ability to hear Him, and write it down here.

GOD LOVE: Who are you praying for today? Become others minded by praying for others needs. God will meet your needs! Help others win and God will help you win.

GOD THOUGHT: What are you choosing to think about today? We should always choose our thoughts!

CONFESSING GOD'S WORD

TEACHING NOTES:

Speaker ____________________

Date ____________________

Topic ____________________

CONFESSING GOD'S WORD:

Say this out loud every day this week!

Revelations 22:13

I am the Alpha and the Omega, the First and the Last, the Beginning and the End.

Politics as Usual?

So we just had an election and we're about to swear in our new President. Now is Taking A Minute gonna get all political? Well, NO, but you know I like to promote thinking, and sometimes a challenge. If you didn't get to vote in this election, you might be able to vote in the next one, so listen up. Who are you thinking of voting for… and why? Today I am asking you to make sure you, number 1, vote. Make sure your voice is heard. Every one of us should stop what we are doing and make sure we vote. This means get registered now! Number 2, vote your conscience. Don't just vote for who everyone else is voting for, or who your family is voting for, or what your political party is, but vote your conscience. Make sure you vote for the individual you really think would be best. Number 3, be educated in who you are voting for. Find out for yourself about each candidate. I say that because the media is not the best source of information. Things on the news and in the papers are painted to promote the candidate they hope will win. Hollywood is pretty twisted in their views too. Find out for yourself who these candidates are, and what they have done. Jesus taught us that only God knows the heart of man, but we can see a glimpse of a person's heart by looking at the fruit. "You will know them by their fruit". So look at what each person has accomplished so far. I know the general trend right now is to say that a candidate's personal life or belief is not important when it comes to making them a leader. That simply is not true. If someone cannot lead themselves successfully, then neither will they lead a country successfully. And there is no question that in the years Israel had a leader who was godly, that the nation was blessed, but when the leader was ungodly, well, it was no good. On that note I would like to announce that I'm running for President. … well, no, probably not.

GOD MAIL: Write down some thoughts you want to share with God.

GOD REPLY: Did you hear any thoughts that you think might be from God? Exercise your ability to hear Him, and write it down here.

GOD LOVE: Who are you praying for today? Become others minded by praying for others needs. God will meet your needs! Help others win and God will help you win.

GOD THOUGHT: What are you choosing to think about today? We should always choose our thoughts!

CONFESSING GOD'S WORD

TEACHING NOTES:

Speaker ____________________

Date ____________________

Topic ____________________

CONFESSING GOD'S WORD:
Say this out loud every day this week!

John 15:5
I am the vine; you are the branches. If a man remains in me and I in him, he will bear much fruit; apart from me you can do nothing.

Livin' and Lovin'

In the book of Ecclesiastes Solomon says, "Do not be overly righteous, a man who fears God will avoid all extremes." Now this is the Bible, so sit up and pay attention. What does he mean by not being overly righteous? Well, you have been made righteous by the blood of Jesus. Jesus' sacrifice for your sins makes you holy, righteous, and blameless. The key is you have to confess your sins to God, and ask Him to forgive you. Make Jesus Lord of your life! So if you are already righteous, how can you be overly righteous? Overly righteous means you think you're more righteous than everyone else. You might start commenting on what everyone else is doing wrong, looking at others and saying, "Oh, I'm not like them. I would never do that." Then you might get all offended and quit going to church. Or you might find yourself making up a bunch of rules that aren't in the Bible, and judging in your heart the people who don't live up to your standards. The scripture also says, "Don't be overly wicked and shorten your life." So it's saying live a good life, but don't get to looking down on others and thinking you're all holy because of how you live. Live right, and part of living right is looking upon others with grace and compassion, and especially love. Remember that those who live in the world and are not followers of Christ just don't know any better, so we cannot get down on them. They will know we are Christians by our love, and they will be won over by our love. You also don't want to start coming against another Christian, because the truth is that God is the protector of His children. Love each other. And love me, because sometimes I feel so all alone. Just kidding!

GOD MAIL: Write down some thoughts you want to share with God.

GOD REPLY: Did you hear any thoughts that you think might be from God? Exercise your ability to hear Him, and write it down here.

GOD LOVE: Who are you praying for today? Become others minded by praying for others needs. God will meet your needs! Help others win and God will help you win.

GOD THOUGHT: What are you choosing to think about today? We should always choose our thoughts!

CONFESSING GOD'S WORD

TEACHING NOTES:

Speaker ____________________

Date ____________________

Topic ____________________

CONFESSING GOD'S WORD:

Say this out loud every day this week!

John 13:35

By this all men will know that you are my disciples, if you love one another.

A Course, Of Course

So the other day we are traveling through downtown Seattle. We were hoofin' it, and without a map. So if we are looking for some place in particular, forget it, cause downtown Seattle's got a lot of stuff to do, and without a map, we are just wandering. There is a coffee café about every 4 feet, and after my eighth cup, I decided it was time to find something else… but what, and where? Well, wandering around is a bit pointless. Now life is a little like that. We can follow a course, or just wander around. The Israelites spent 40 years wandering around in the desert, but that was not God's plan. God wanted them to cross over into the land He had promised them. A good and spacious land, flowing with milk and honey, where they would live in cities that they did not have to build, and drink from wells that they did not have to dig. According to God's plan for them, life would be full of abundance, more than they needed. When you have more than you need is finally when you can give some away. This is a picture of how we can choose to live today in our Christian walk, we can wander around in the desert, just barely getting our needs met, just enough to pay the bills, or we can go into His promised land for us. Now crossing over is going to take faith and courage. It starts with living on course, living the plan that God has for you. It means getting your map. Faith comes by hearing God's Word, so start hearing it. Now you should read it too, but I also suggest finding a church that teaches God's word. That's the map. It's how you find your course. God has a great life planned for you, but you have to believe it, and fight for it. Or you can wander in the desert.

GOD MAIL: Write down some thoughts you want to share with God.

GOD REPLY: Did you hear any thoughts that you think might be from God? Exercise your ability to hear Him, and write it down here.

GOD LOVE: Who are you praying for today? Become others minded by praying for others needs. God will meet your needs! Help others win and God will help you win.

GOD THOUGHT: What are you choosing to think about today? We should always choose our thoughts!

CONFESSING GOD'S WORD

TEACHING NOTES:

Speaker ____________________

Date ____________________

Topic ____________________

CONFESSING GOD'S WORD:

Say this out loud every day this week!

Jeremiah 29:11

For I know the plans I have for you," declares the LORD, "plans to prosper you and not to harm you, plans to give you hope and a future..."

Possessed

Well Joshua and the Israelites are in the Promised Land now, but there are other nations still living there. He crossed the Jordan because he believed that God didn't want them to live in the desert anymore, but had a better life planned! So God tells them to dispossess the nations, and possess the land. Now this is a picture of your Christian walk. God has many promises for you, and just as Joshua took the land one city at a time, so you also receive God's promises one city at a time. You must dispossess the city before you can possess it. Which means you have to get rid of something before you get something. What you are receiving is the promise of God, but you must rid yourself of something first. So what are some things you could rid yourself of? Well, how about fear, or envy, how about unforgiveness? Are you offended with someone? Are you mad at all them church folk? What can you get rid of? Clean out the house a little bit and make some room for a promise that God has for you. Jesus supplied the promise and it is free, but you have to believe and receive it. Now, to give you an example, the Cannanites were a nation that Joshua had to overcome. In fact all of the nations in the land in one way or another descended from the Canannites, including the Hivites, the Jebusites, the Perazites, and probably some termites, etc… The word Canannites means perversion. These were the same people who lived in Sodom and Gomorrah. So God was showing us a picture that we have to get rid of the perversion in our life. Perversion is when we take something that God intended for good, and twist it into something that will do us harm. But when we get rid of perversion, we find enjoyment in what God originally intended for our pleasure. And then we create space in our life for God's promise to become a reality. And that can't be bad.

GOD MAIL: Write down some thoughts you want to share with God.

GOD REPLY: Did you hear any thoughts that you think might be from God? Exercise your ability to hear Him, and write it down here.

GOD LOVE: Who are you praying for today? Become others minded by praying for others needs. God will meet your needs! Help others win and God will help you win.

GOD THOUGHT: What are you choosing to think about today? We should always choose our thoughts!

CONFESSING GOD'S WORD

TEACHING NOTES:

Speaker ____________________

Date ____________________

Topic ____________________

CONFESSING GOD'S WORD:

Say this out loud every day this week!

Romans 12:2

Do not conform any longer to the pattern of this world, but be transformed by the renewing of your mind. Then you will be able to test and approve what God's will is—his good, pleasing and perfect will.

What's in Your Wallet?

Let's talk about money. It pays for our cars, our gas, rent, school, insurance, clothes… bills, bills, bills. So, in the New Testament Paul is asking the church of Corinth to send in some dough to help with the cause of church planting and spreading the gospel, missionary and apostle work. He is asking the church to send some money over, and here's what he says in 2 Corinthians 8:9: "For you know the grace of our Lord Jesus Christ, that though He was rich, yet for your sakes, He became poor, so that you through His poverty might become rich." It's important here to grasp that this context of the scripture is in fact referring to money, not spiritual wealth, but, ladies and gentlemen, he's talking about moola, money, quid, a grip, cha ching. OHH WAIT, the Bible talking about money? Wait, that's wrong. Well, some people abuse money, or trust in it like it's their God, or love money. Money isn't a thing you can love; it's a tool, and like all tools, it can be used for good or bad. One guy might use a key to scratch someone else's car. That doesn't make keys bad. I use my keys to open stuff. Money is a tool. Now, Jesus became poor so that you might be rich. Jesus became poor on the cross, stripped of everything, even His clothes, and nailed to a cross where He died. Well, our poverty – yours and mine – died with Him on the cross. Now Jesus didn't become poor so you could own way more junk than you need, junk that just wears out. He wants you to have more than you need so that you can give it away. It takes money to spread the gospel to the nations, to feed the widow, to give housing to the orphans. Now if we allow God to make us prosperous, and then use that wealth to further the kingdom of God, that's what Paul was talking about. So send me your money. Ha ha, just kidding. Give it to the storehouse, your church.

GOD MAIL: Write down some thoughts you want to share with God.

GOD REPLY: Did you hear any thoughts that you think might be from God? Exercise your ability to hear Him, and write it down here.

GOD LOVE: Who are you praying for today? Become others minded by praying for others needs. God will meet your needs! Help others win and God will help you win.

GOD THOUGHT: What are you choosing to think about today? We should always choose our thoughts!

CONFESSING GOD'S WORD

TEACHING NOTES:

Speaker ________________

Date ________________

Topic ________________

CONFESSING GOD'S WORD:

Say this out loud every day this week!

2 Corinthians 8:9

For you know the grace of our Lord Jesus Christ, that though he was rich, yet for your sakes he became poor, so that you through his poverty might become rich.

When Opportunity Knocks

In Mark 16:15, Jesus said, "Go into all the world and preach the good news to all creation." Well what's the good news? The good news is that salvation is free to anyone who will accept Jesus Christ as the son of God who died for all sin and make him Lord and Savior of his or her life. You know, you've tried to do life your way for awhile. Now give Jesus your life and watch Him go. So, we are supposed to be telling people about this. He said to preach it to all creation. Well, for some that may mean traveling to Zimbabwe, but if everyone goes to Zimbabe, then who is going to spread it in your neighborhood? Now a real recent trend in society is telling us that each person's faith is a private thing, and we shouldn't try and impose our faith on someone else. You know, let people believe what they want to believe. But be careful of this kind of thinking. Jesus instructed us to tell others about Him; others: the whole world, all of creation. Now I'm not saying that we should all be at the street corner yelling at some guy that he is destined to burn forever. What I'm saying is that people need to hear the news. They need to hear that God, Who created them, loves them and sent His only Son to die for them. So many have not received Christ, and God, to them, is this far away person who is randomly mean to the world. People need to hear that God is good and that He is our Father if we will receive Him. People need to hear how Jesus has changed you, what you were like before, and how you're different now. Ask God to give you an opportunity to share the good news. If someone is telling you about a problem, ask them if you can pray for them. Give to others, love others, and these doors will begin to open, and you can be obedient to this command that Jesus has given us.

GOD MAIL: Write down some thoughts you want to share with God.

___

GOD REPLY: Did you hear any thoughts that you think might be from God? Exercise your ability to hear Him, and write it down here.

GOD LOVE: Who are you praying for today? Become others minded by praying for others needs. God will meet your needs! Help others win and God will help you win.

GOD THOUGHT: What are you choosing to think about today? We should always choose our thoughts!

CONFESSING GOD'S WORD

TEACHING NOTES:

Speaker ____________________

Date ____________________

Topic ____________________

CONFESSING GOD'S WORD:

Say this out loud every day this week!

Mark 16:15

He said to them, "Go into all the world and preach the good news to all creation.

First Things First

Look at Genesis 1:28. The first thing God does and says after He creates man… It says, "God blessed them and said to them, be fruitful, and increase in number, fill the earth and subdue it." So what was the first thing He did? He blessed them. Now we don't use the word blessed much in every day circles, so if you're wondering what it means, and you're thinking, "Well if God blessed me it would be with a red Ferarri." Well, that's not what he did for Adam. When God blessed man, He gave man the ability to become successful and prosperous. He didn't give him a thing, like a brand new elephant. He gave him an ability. Now 6,000 years later you still have that ability through Jesus Christ. You are blessed. That initial blessing is very important to remember, because God has put certain other abilities within you to help you make a real difference on earth. There are hidden desires and talents within you that God will reveal in season, and that blessing that He gave you at the beginning of time is going to be critical in your accomplishing, finishing and winning your destiny. With that in mind, God said we are to "Subdue the earth". Subdue the earth means to be in charge of the earth. God wants you to be in charge around here. Well that makes sense, because as you gain more and more authority on earth, you gain more and more influence and ability to make changes, to help more people. This was the first thing God did after creating us. He gave us the ability to make a difference on this planet, and the authority to accomplish it! Well that's a lot to do, so we all better get going!

GOD MAIL: Write down some thoughts you want to share with God.

GOD REPLY: Did you hear any thoughts that you think might be from God? Exercise your ability to hear Him, and write it down here.

GOD LOVE: Who are you praying for today? Become others minded by praying for others needs. God will meet your needs! Help others win and God will help you win.

GOD THOUGHT: What are you choosing to think about today? We should always choose our thoughts!

CONFESSING GOD'S WORD

TEACHING NOTES:

Speaker ____________________

Date ____________________

Topic ____________________

CONFESSING GOD'S WORD:

Say this out loud every day this week!

Genesis 1:26

Then God said, "Let us make man in our image, in our likeness, and let them rule over the fish of the sea and the birds of the air, over the livestock, over all the earth, [a] and over all the creatures that move along the ground."

You Want Anything Else With That Chicken?

What are your deepest desires? You know that we have many desires deep within us, and the ones that get stirred up in us are the ones that drive us to a lot of the things we do. Television recognizes this power, and so they show us the food that looks oh, so good, or the car that we really want, because they know it works. All too often we allow random input into our minds that stirs our desires up, and then we go in all different directions. But a righteous man's steps are ordered of the Lord. God has a very specific road for us to follow. In Colossions 3:2, the Scripture says, "Set your affections on things above, not on earthly things." Affections here refers to that moment when our desire meets with fulfillment, or the moment you actually eat that oh, so good looking food that you were thinking about. God wants us to set the desire on things above. This means to set your goals higher, to reach for the stars, to dream big. God wants to give you the deep desires of your heart that will point you to your destiny. All too often we set our desires too low. I mean, you want that chicken meal you saw on T.V., but anyone can buy a chicken meal. Instead, set your desire on something that you will need God to help you accomplish. When our affections are set on earthly things, remember that the earth is full of dirt, and your body is made of dirt, so then everything just ends up all dirty. Now Jesus has washed you up. So, set your affections on the stars, and let the good desires in your heart drive you down the right road.

GOD MAIL: Write down some thoughts you want to share with God.

GOD REPLY: Did you hear any thoughts that you think might be from God? Exercise your ability to hear Him, and write it down here.

GOD LOVE: Who are you praying for today? Become others minded by praying for others needs. God will meet your needs! Help others win and God will help you win.

GOD THOUGHT: What are you choosing to think about today? We should always choose our thoughts!

CONFESSING GOD'S WORD

TEACHING NOTES:

Speaker ______________________

Date ______________________

Topic ______________________

CONFESSING GOD'S WORD:

Say this out loud every day this week!

Psalms 37:4

Delight yourself in the LORD and he will give you the desires of your heart.

Being the King's Kid

Romans 8:16 says that the Spirit himself testifies with our spirit that we are God's children. Galatians 3:26 says, "You are all sons of God through faith in Christ Jesus." Now God is, well, He is God. Of all the people running the show on this planet, the kings, prime ministers, presidents, ali babwas or whatever, our world leaders cannot compare to the authority of God Who is the Creator of all. And you, my friend, are a son of God. Not the Son of God, but an adopted son of God through Jesus Christ. Now if you're the president's kid, you probably get some special privileges, right? Free white house tours, secret service protection… Or if you're the son of a king, or daughter of the king, cuz the scripture term "sons" means mankind, which definitely includes the women, that would make you a prince, or a princess… This means a castle, with a moat. And Jesus isn't just a king, He's the King of Kings according to Revelation Chapter 19. Billy Graham was asked once if he gets nervous meeting with so many world leaders about God, and his reply was, "I just remember that I am an Ambassador for the greatest King of all, so there is no need to be nervous." Wherever you go remember that you are royalty in the Kingdom of God, that you represent the Most High, and that God doesn't just call you royalty, He treats you like royalty. And He is a great Father, the best Dad a person could ever have, a Father that gives the richest blessings to His children, like health, love, streets of gold, and a great chariot. Now I don't need a chariot, and the street outside my house is still your typical black top, but I'll go out and check every day. Is it gold yet? Nope. Maybe tomorrow.

GOD MAIL: Write down some thoughts you want to share with God.

GOD REPLY: Did you hear any thoughts that you think might be from God? Exercise your ability to hear Him, and write it down here.

GOD LOVE: Who are you praying for today? Become others minded by praying for others needs. God will meet your needs! Help others win and God will help you win.

GOD THOUGHT: What are you choosing to think about today? We should always choose our thoughts!

CONFESSING GOD'S WORD

TEACHING NOTES:

Speaker ________________

Date ________________

Topic ________________

CONFESSING GOD'S WORD:

Say this out loud every day this week!

1 Peter 2:9

But you are a chosen people, a royal priesthood, a holy nation, a people belonging to God, that you may declare the praises of him who called you out of darkness into his wonderful light.

Amazing Grace

Galatians 2:21 says, "I do not set aside the grace of God, for if righteousness could be gained through the law, Christ died for nothing!" A few keys here, first - the goal is to attain righteousness. Righteousness means that when God looks at your life He's like, "Yeah, you're holy, blameless, perfect." So you're thinking, "Well, that's not me. I don't obey all the rules." Well, I have a great answer for that. Righteousness has nothing to do with the rules. The scripture said that righteousness cannot be gained through the law, which is "the rules." Most people are thinking that they can't talk to God because of the mistakes they have made. They distance themselves from God. Or that God won't answer my prayers because I'm not good enough. God said He would never leave you nor forsake you. Never!! We are all trying to be good enough, but we can't possibly obey all the rules. God knows that about us, so He says if we would just believe in Jesus and what He did, then ask God to forgive us for the places we mess up, that He will forgive us and even forget about it. Does that mean you should just have a big sin fest? Of course not, instead we are to live our lives with integrity and character because we are in debt to what Jesus did for us. He died for our sins. We have to let the grace of God teach us to live better! But obeying the rules or not obeying the rules doesn't change what God has promised for you, or whether or not He is listening to your prayers. Jesus came so that you could have a relationship with God without obeying all the rules. And if you are obeying all the rules, like me, then good job. Oops, that was me lying... eee.

GOD MAIL: Write down some thoughts you want to share with God.

GOD REPLY: Did you hear any thoughts that you think might be from God? Exercise your ability to hear Him, and write it down here.

GOD LOVE: Who are you praying for today? Become others minded by praying for others needs. God will meet your needs! Help others win and God will help you win.

GOD THOUGHT: What are you choosing to think about today? We should always choose our thoughts!

CONFESSING GOD'S WORD

TEACHING NOTES:

Speaker ______________________

Date ______________________

Topic ______________________

CONFESSING GOD'S WORD:

Say this out loud every day this week!

Romans 8:39

Neither height nor depth, nor anything else in all creation, will be able to separate us from the love of God that is in Christ Jesus our Lord.

Get in the Game

In the New Testament the Church is referred to 112 times. It is the body of people where the name of the Lord dwells, a place where those who believe in Christ come together, a place of gathering. It is the storehouse, where the Word of God, which is food, comes out and feeds the people. The Church is referred to as the Body of Christ and as the bride of Christ. Now my wife is pretty important to me, so how important is the Church to Jesus? Most of the books in the New Testament were letters written to churches, not to individuals, describing God's most precious promised inheritance. I Timothy 3:15 says, "God's household… is the church of the living God, the pillar and foundation of the truth." So not being in a church is like being homeless in God's kingdom. Say what you want about the Church but the Bible tells us it is the pillar and foundation of truth, and God's Word is the real truth. Now I know there's a trend to redefine church so that people are comfortable not going. Let's make it a drive-thru church, or just chillin' at home. But the intent of the church is to bring people together into the unity of faith so that we can really impact this world. It's a team effort, and there are people on the team who do not attend practice or come to the game. To them I say, "Hey! Get in the game, we need you, we want church to be relevant, full of truth, grace, love and the Word of God." And if you say, "Well, I just don't enjoy going to church," then I would say, "Well, go anyway; not everything you do has to be fun." And I'll bet you'll start enjoying it when you make the commitment!!

GOD MAIL: Write down some thoughts you want to share with God.

GOD REPLY: Did you hear any thoughts that you think might be from God? Exercise your ability to hear Him, and write it down here.

GOD LOVE: Who are you praying for today? Become others minded by praying for others needs. God will meet your needs! Help others win and God will help you win.

GOD THOUGHT: What are you choosing to think about today? We should always choose our thoughts!

CONFESSING GOD'S WORD

TEACHING NOTES:

Speaker ____________________

Date ____________________

Topic ____________________

CONFESSING GOD'S WORD:

Say this out loud every day this week!

Psalms 92:13

Planted in the house of the LORD, they will flourish in the courts of our God.

A Test? Today?

In Matthew 4:7, Satan takes Jesus up to the highest point of the temple and says, “Hey jump off and the angels will catch you…” So Jesus says, “It is written: ‘Do not put the Lord your God to the test.’“ But then Malachi 3:10 tells us, when asking us to make sure we give God 10% of our income as our tithes, God says, “Test me in this, see if I will not throw open the windows of heaven and pour out so much blessing you will be unable to contain it.” So in one scripture it says, don’t put God to the test, and then in a different one it says its okay to test God. So which is it? Well, you can test God when it comes to His principles and blessings. Like tithing, He is saying, “If you give Me what is Mine, 10%, then watch and see what happens. You are going to have more in the end. In fact, I’ll work it out so that you have more than you can hold.” And obviously He is talking about money. The kind of test that Jesus is saying we should not put God to, is throwing yourself into danger and asking God to save you. Like jumping off a building and asking God to catch you, or walking on hot coals and asking God to not make them burn. God isn’t into that sort of thing. Someone might quit working and ask God to meet their needs, but that isn’t a God-principle. God’s word says that if you don’t work, you don’t eat. So when they turn off the electricity, don’t blame God, just go get a job. But the kind of test that activates God’s principles and blessings, hey, He’s okay with that. Like if you don’t believe in Christ, I would say to take this test: Choose to receive him into your heart, confess that Jesus is Lord out loud Be sincere about your decision, and watch your life begin to change. Watch the freedom you feel, the love. Test God in this and see if you don’t get to go to heaven too. And I’ll see ya there!

GOD MAIL: Write down some thoughts you want to share with God.

GOD REPLY: Did you hear any thoughts that you think might be from God? Exercise your ability to hear Him, and write it down here.

GOD LOVE: Who are you praying for today? Become others minded by praying for others needs. God will meet your needs! Help others win and God will help you win.

GOD THOUGHT: What are you choosing to think about today? We should always choose our thoughts!

CONFESSING GOD'S WORD

TEACHING NOTES:

Speaker ______________________

Date ______________________

Topic ______________________

CONFESSING GOD'S WORD:

Say this out loud every day this week!

Joshua 1:8

Do not let this Book of the Law depart from your mouth; meditate on it day and night, so that you may be careful to do everything written in it. Then you will be prosperous and successful.

True That

Liar, liar pants on fire. Now I'm not sure why your pants would catch fire if you lie, I think it just rhymes. I've never actually seen it happen. Hey, what happened to your jeans? Yeah, that. I was telling my boss why I was late, and boom, my pants caught fire. But we are a society of truth-stretching and exaggeration. Or sometimes we leave key elements out. "Sorry I'm late. My alarm didn't go off." Of course we leave out the fact that we broke it the morning before by chucking it across the room. And your little stretches and exaggerations mess with people's ability to trust you, especially those closest to you. Like when you tell your friends, "Oh, just tell Jimmy that I'm not feeling well." And so your friends tell Jimmy that, and then they think, "Hey, you're a liar." And then your pants catch on fire… So then when we are really telling the truth we say, "No really, I promise, I swear," which is letting everyone know that, "Yeah normally I lie, but not this time because I'm saying, 'I promise.'" Now I'm not trying to get down on you, but I do want you to hear this. Jesus said to not do all this promising stuff. He said in Matthew 5 to "simply let your 'yes' be 'yes' and your 'no' be 'no.'" He's teaching us about truth. The Word of God is so powerful because it is always true. Now your words have the ability to be powerful, the power of life and death are in your tongue. So let every word you speak be the truth as you know it, even if it means getting yourself in trouble. Then watch yourself begin to grow. I promise, I mean…hmmm.

GOD MAIL: Write down some thoughts you want to share with God.

GOD REPLY: Did you hear any thoughts that you think might be from God? Exercise your ability to hear Him, and write it down here.

GOD LOVE: Who are you praying for today? Become others minded by praying for others needs. God will meet your needs! Help others win and God will help you win.

GOD THOUGHT: What are you choosing to think about today? We should always choose our thoughts!

CONFESSING GOD'S WORD

TEACHING NOTES:

Speaker ____________________

Date ____________________

Topic ____________________

CONFESSING GOD'S WORD:

Say this out loud every day this week!

Proverbs 24:26

An honest answer is like a kiss on the lips.

Good Advice

A penny saved is a penny earned. But you know, what do you do with that penny, and does God really want us to be cheap with each other? How about, be ye a lender nor a borrower be. Is that a scripture? No! God says in Deuteronomy 28 that He wants to bless you so that you would lend to entire nations. And that would make you a lender. So there are some worldly wisdoms and sayings, even stories that we have heard that don't always agree with the scripture. Like the Rock-a-Bye Baby song. I don't think it's ever going to be biblical for you to put a newborn baby in a cradle in a tree top, and then sing a song about the baby falling out of the tree. What kind of weirdos are we dealing with here? I Timothy 4:7, "Have nothing to do with godless myths and old wives tales; rather, train yourself to be godly." We train ourselves by taking advice from God's Word, and reconciling everything that we know and who we are, using the wisdom God has provided. I mean sure, there are lots of really smart things that really smart people say, but what if they are wrong? What if what worked for them isn't going to work for you? So then you could wander through the world blind just trying to figure everything out for yourself by making a whole mess of mistakes and learning from them, or, you could allow the Word of God to train you. There are plenty of people in the Bible making mistakes you can learn from. Like when Moses says, "Who am I?" He was feeling a little less than equipped for the task. But then, he let God train him, and look what he did. And look what you can do!

GOD MAIL: Write down some thoughts you want to share with God.

GOD REPLY: Did you hear any thoughts that you think might be from God? Exercise your ability to hear Him, and write it down here.

GOD LOVE: Who are you praying for today? Become others minded by praying for others needs. God will meet your needs! Help others win and God will help you win.

GOD THOUGHT: What are you choosing to think about today? We should always choose our thoughts!

CONFESSING GOD'S WORD

TEACHING NOTES:

Speaker ____________________

Date ____________________

Topic ____________________

CONFESSING GOD'S WORD:

Say this out loud every day this week!

2 Timothy 3:16

All Scripture is God-breathed and is useful for teaching, rebuking, correcting and training in righteousness,

Mission Control

You know that moment when your buttons have all been pushed and you flip out and lose control? Or have you ever determined that you were gonna eat better, and then you cave and eat some thing you shouldn't, lose control? So, I Titus 2:6 says, "Encourage the young men to be self controlled." Well that sounds easy. Hey, don't lose your temper anymore, ever again. Don't ever do anything mean or wrong ever again. It's easy, eh? Well, not that easy. Controlling yourself is difficult. I mean it is yourself, which indicates ownership, you are actually in charge of the self that is yours, but sometimes it forgets, ya know? Well, if I keep reading, I get a little secret about learning self control. It goes on to say, "In everything set them an example by doing what is good." Ah ha. The focus isn't placed on what you need to STOP doing here, but what you need to DO. It is an action, not a stopping of an action. According to this, if you focus on the good things that you can do, like giving to someone, helping others, serving in your church, obeying those in authority, you know, loving other people, and finding ways to work with all your heart towards those things that the Lord has for you, then the whole self control thing should just start clicking along. Maybe we spend so much time focusing on trying to have more self control that when we mess up, we feel like failures. According to this scripture though, the real task at hand is becoming an example to others of the good things that we can accomplish if we apply ourselves. I mean, what really got Paul turned around was his obedience to Christ in what he was going to accomplish. And that can be you too!

GOD MAIL: Write down some thoughts you want to share with God.

GOD REPLY: Did you hear any thoughts that you think might be from God? Exercise your ability to hear Him, and write it down here.

GOD LOVE: Who are you praying for today? Become others minded by praying for others needs. God will meet your needs! Help others win and God will help you win.

GOD THOUGHT: What are you choosing to think about today? We should always choose our thoughts!

CONFESSING GOD'S WORD

TEACHING NOTES:

Speaker ____________________

Date ____________________

Topic ____________________

CONFESSING GOD'S WORD:

Say this out loud every day this week!

Psalms 143:10

Teach me to do your will, for you are my God; may your good Spirit lead me on level ground.

Meet, Know, Grow

Hey, you know me, right? Well, no, not really. I mean, most of you have no idea what I look like. Let's be honest, we've never met probably. Or if I have met you, I apologize cuz right now your name escapes me. But I like you. So okay, let's agree you don't know me, but you have to agree as well that I exist. I mean, if I didn't exist, then you wouldn't be reading this right now. And that has nothing to do with whether you believe in me or not, these words just simply wouldn't be on this page. So okay, you believe in me, but you don't know me. Right? Now, let me ask you this... Do you believe in God? Okay, now the second question, do you know God? Have you ever met? Believing in God is the starting point. You see, even the devil and his staff believe in God. Do you know God? I was talking to a guy the other day standing in line and he said that he used to believe in God, but now he doesn't. So I said, "Well the problem is you've never met God." I went on to explain that after you meet God, you have to pursue God to get to know Him. God says if you seek me, you'll find me. So this guy says, "Well how does a person meet God?" And I said, "I'm so glad you asked me that. The problem is, I can't introduce Him to you. Only His Son Jesus can." Jesus said, "No one comes to the Father except through me." Jesus has made the way. All you have to do is put your faith in Jesus, the only Son of God who died for your sins, and rose from the dead. And then you can say, "Hey God, what's up?" And don't be surprised if somehow you know He replies, "I'm glad you asked me that. I've got something for you..." Then get ready.

GOD MAIL: Write down some thoughts you want to share with God.

GOD REPLY: Did you hear any thoughts that you think might be from God? Exercise your ability to hear Him, and write it down here.

GOD LOVE: Who are you praying for today? Become others minded by praying for others needs. God will meet your needs! Help others win and God will help you win.

GOD THOUGHT: What are you choosing to think about today? We should always choose our thoughts!

CONFESSING GOD'S WORD

TEACHING NOTES:

Speaker ______________________

Date ______________________

Topic ______________________

CONFESSING GOD'S WORD:

Say this out loud every day this week!

Jeremiah 29:13

You will seek me and find me when you seek me with all your heart.

One is the Loneliest Number

You ever feel alone? I mean really alone. No matter how much money you have, or your social status, you can be alone. Whether you have two loving parents, or no parents, family, or none, loneliness doesn't care about these kinds of things. You can be surrounded by people, and still feel alone. And there are lots of songs about being lonely; I googled it and found 52 different songs about loneliness. But I don't think singing about loneliness, or listening to depressing songs, will help you with loneliness. Well, good news for the lonely: Jehovah Shammah is one of the names of God, which means The Lord God Ever Present. So remember this, wherever you go, God is there. Deuteronomy 31:6 says, "He will never leave you." That's right. Right in the middle of tragedy, God is there to give you comfort, and when trouble comes, Jesus is in the boat with you, waiting for you to call on Him to help you through. When you get mad at someone, God is there to help you forgive, and when you feel all out of love, God has some more love for you. So even when you call around and no one is answering their phone, and you're thinking, "Well, I'm alone, who can I talk to?" Well, you could talk to God. In fact, you could stop reading this right now and talk to God. He's got something really cool He wants to say to you, I'll bet. Cuz you know, He's God, so it's probably a lot better than what I'm saying.

GOD MAIL: Write down some thoughts you want to share with God.

GOD REPLY: Did you hear any thoughts that you think might be from God? Exercise your ability to hear Him, and write it down here.

GOD LOVE: Who are you praying for today? Become others minded by praying for others needs. God will meet your needs! Help others win and God will help you win.

GOD THOUGHT: What are you choosing to think about today? We should always choose our thoughts!

CONFESSING GOD'S WORD

TEACHING NOTES:

Speaker ____________________

Date ____________________

Topic ____________________

CONFESSING GOD'S WORD:

Say this out loud every day this week!

Psalm 73:23

Yet I am always with you; you hold me by my right hand.

Road Signs

Psalms 119:97 says, "Oh, how I love your law! I meditate on it all day long." Okay, well, it's in the Bible so we better learn from it. How many of you have gone by a speed limit sign that says 45, and you're doing 50? My kids are all, "Hey, dad, you're speeding." Now the speed limit law is a law in my state that tells me how fast I can go. It's a law, but I don't love the law. I should obey it, but do I love it? I mean, am I all, "Man, look at that stop sign. That's a great law, look how it makes me stop. Wow, I'm gonna think about it all day." Now I should obey it so I don't get in a wreck and hurt someone, but am I in love with the law? Now God has some principles that are in place in this world. The principles look like this: if I do something wrong, then things aren't going to go well for me. God wants his children to be successful, and He wants us to be blessed, and He has given us principles for us to live by. He has asked us to love one another, to lay down our lives for others, and to love him with all of our heart. The Bible here is telling us that we should learn all of God's principles, and love them, to recognize that they are in fact the road to us finding ourselves safely in God's arms. And maybe if we fell in love with God's words, and thought about His Words daily, life would get a bit easier, and maybe we would find ourselves in less, um, wrecks. Maybe we would see that stop sign when we start down the wrong road, or are a little out of control. I'll bet we'd find ourselves in a better place.... And who couldn't use that?

GOD MAIL: Write down some thoughts you want to share with God.

GOD REPLY: Did you hear any thoughts that you think might be from God? Exercise your ability to hear Him, and write it down here.

GOD LOVE: Who are you praying for today? Become others minded by praying for others needs. God will meet your needs! Help others win and God will help you win.

GOD THOUGHT: What are you choosing to think about today? We should always choose our thoughts!

CONFESSING GOD'S WORD

TEACHING NOTES:

Speaker ______________________

Date ______________________

Topic ______________________

CONFESSING GOD'S WORD:

Say this out loud every day this week!

Psalms 18:22

All his laws are before me; I have not turned away from his decrees.

Going Up?

My very first apartment was upstairs on the second floor of the building, and there was no elevator. So every day, it's up and down the stairs. K, no big deal, except when you're trying to move a sectional couch up the stairs. I tried to figure out other ways to get up to the apartment, but the truth was, there was no other way. There was one set of stairs, and that was it. The Kingdom of Heaven is very much the same. Well, my apartment certainly wasn't heaven, it was smaller, and there were no streets of gold, but the way to heaven is similar. Jesus said, "I am the way the truth and the life. No one comes to the Father except through me." So Jesus made it very clear: If you decide to choose God in your lifetime, you have to receive Jesus. There are no secret other elevators, there's no special pulley system around Jesus. You can't use a make shift trampoline, or, according to the kid's praise song, you can't get to heaven in a Kleenex box. Although, if someone tried, I would have to commend them on ingenuity. According to this scripture, the truth, God's Word, right from Jesus' very own mouth, you have to believe in Jesus Christ if you wish to hang in that apartment upstairs in the sweet by and by. If you are thinking, "Hey, I'm looking forward to walking through those pearly gates, but I'm gonna get there by taking the bus instead of getting on the Jesus Glory Train," then I have one suggestion: Bring something cold to drink. God is our Creator, and He wants to know you, and He has told you the way, and it is the only way. It is through His Son Jesus who died for you and rose again, and belief in Him is your ticket. Tickets, please…

GOD MAIL: Write down some thoughts you want to share with God.

GOD REPLY: Did you hear any thoughts that you think might be from God? Exercise your ability to hear Him, and write it down here.

GOD LOVE: Who are you praying for today? Become others minded by praying for others needs. God will meet your needs! Help others win and God will help you win.

GOD THOUGHT: What are you choosing to think about today? We should always choose our thoughts!

CONFESSING GOD'S WORD

TEACHING NOTES:

Speaker ____________________

Date ____________________

Topic ____________________

CONFESSING GOD'S WORD:

Say this out loud every day this week!

John 14:26

But the Counselor, the Holy Spirit, whom the Father will send in my name, will teach you all things and will remind you of everything I have said to you.

Battle Ready

Proverbs 21:31:The horse is made ready for the day of battle, but victory rests with the Lord. So, you have battles in your day, your week, and your life. Your battle could be with your emotions, your addictions, or in your mind. Your battle may be at school, or with your parents, your in-laws, or your job. You could have a battle going on with money, like you are out of it and you have some bills to pay, or a battle with your health. Whatever your battle is, the victory rests with the Lord. That battle is the Lord's, so what do you need to do? What is your part of the battle? This scripture says you have to make the horse ready for battle. That's your part. You probably don't need to go and get a real horse, some armor, maybe a chariot you could buy on eBay, and one of those cool horse helmets. I'm thinking if you bring a horse to school it's going to be a little weird for everyone, especially if you take the time to dress him up like a gladiator. Readying the horse for battle means simply that you are prepared for the fight. In a real battle you would want to do some training, prepare mentally, and make sure the tools for battle were all ready to go. You would want to do everything you know to do so that you were ready to fight. And that is what God is saying to us today, in this scripture. He's saying, "Rest assured that I've got your back, the battle and the victory rest with Me, but you need to do everything you know to do." If you are praying for healing in your body, you should get the horse ready too, like eating right, exercising maybe, going to the doctor. Now you don't put your trust in the doctor, or the food you eat, your trust remains with God. We know, though, that faith without works is dead, so have faith in God, and get up and get going on some work, too. Feed the horse.

GOD MAIL: Write down some thoughts you want to share with God.

GOD REPLY: Did you hear any thoughts that you think might be from God? Exercise your ability to hear Him, and write it down here.

GOD LOVE: Who are you praying for today? Become others minded by praying for others needs. God will meet your needs! Help others win and God will help you win.

GOD THOUGHT: What are you choosing to think about today? We should always choose our thoughts!

CONFESSING GOD'S WORD

TEACHING NOTES:

Speaker ____________________

Date ____________________

Topic ____________________

CONFESSING GOD'S WORD:

Say this out loud every day this week!

Psalms 55:18

He ransoms me unharmed from the battle waged against me, even though many oppose me.

Salty is Good

In I Corinthians 5:6 Paul asks this question, "Don't you know that a little yeast works through the whole batch of dough?" By yeast he's talking about bad influence. And by dough he's talking about you and me. Now, yeast is a bacteria. In it's fundamental nature it is in the fungus family. Right after the Passover the Israelites would eat bread made without yeast. Jesus represents the Passover lamb, and was crucified on the day of the Passover feast. He also is the Bread of Life, but that bread is without yeast, that is, it is sinless, just as Jesus was sinless. God wants us to surround ourselves with positive influence and not negative influence. Now the question is… do we have yeast in our house? Are we around bad influences? You may have Christian friends who influence you in the wrong direction. Or even people who don't know Christ who really pull you down. You can change this by becoming the influencer in that person's life. Jesus told us that we are the salt of the earth. Salt is an influencer, it influences food, and it kills germs and bacteria. In fact, salt kills yeast. God wants the good influencers in your life to replace the bad influencers in your life, and for you to become salt to this earth. When Moses parted the Red Sea, the water caved back in over the Egyptians and drowned them all. The Egyptians were yeast, bad influencers who had enslaved the Israelites, just like sin makes us slaves, but God wants you to be free. And here's a little known fact, the Red Sea is one of the saltiest bodies of water in the world, with more salt in it than the ocean. You may need a flood of salt water in your life to get you free. Get in church and be surrounded by positive people and positive influence!!

GOD MAIL: Write down some thoughts you want to share with God.

GOD REPLY: Did you hear any thoughts that you think might be from God? Exercise your ability to hear Him, and write it down here.

GOD LOVE: Who are you praying for today? Become others minded by praying for others needs. God will meet your needs! Help others win and God will help you win.

GOD THOUGHT: What are you choosing to think about today? We should always choose our thoughts!

CONFESSING GOD'S WORD

TEACHING NOTES:

Speaker ____________________

Date ____________________

Topic ____________________

CONFESSING GOD'S WORD:

Say this out loud every day this week!

1 Corinthians 15:33

Do not be misled: "Bad company corrupts good character."

Howdy, Neighbor

Ahh, love your neighbor as yourself. Go next door and give them some cookies you baked. Loving your neighbor is a command, and in Luke 10:29, a man asked Jesus "Who is my neighbor?" So someone makes you mad and you yell at 'em, show them what's up, right? And that's okay? You're all, "Well this person doesn't live in my neighborhood, I'm good." Jesus describes your neighbor in His answer as the person in your life that you would like least of all. He describes the story of the Good Samaritan. It's important to know that Samaritans and Jews did not associate with one another. In the story it is the Samaritan who stops and helps a Jew who had been beaten and left for dead. The Samaritan recognizes that his neighbors extended beyond culture, color, race, or social status, but knew to love mankind as God's creation. Sometimes we don't like people cuz they are different from us, from another place, or they look different or speak different. Two gangs of people kill each other because they have different gang names. Jesus brought us a message of unifying, not dividing. I don't think this Samaritan was concerned with the Jews' political views, history, background, what he did for a living, or his spiritual status. He didn't ask him if he was a nice person. He helped not because of who the Jew was, but because the Jew existed. He didn't see separation, he saw unity. And although they were so different, they were neighbors, both living together on the same planet. Let's follow this message of Christ. Down with division, do away with hate, be loving and accepting of all.

GOD MAIL: Write down some thoughts you want to share with God.

GOD REPLY: Did you hear any thoughts that you think might be from God? Exercise your ability to hear Him, and write it down here.

GOD LOVE: Who are you praying for today? Become others minded by praying for others needs. God will meet your needs! Help others win and God will help you win.

GOD THOUGHT: What are you choosing to think about today? We should always choose our thoughts!

CONFESSING GOD'S WORD

TEACHING NOTES:

Speaker ____________________

Date ____________________

Topic ____________________

CONFESSING GOD'S WORD:

Say this out loud every day this week!

Luke 6:35

But love your enemies, do good to them, and lend to them without expecting to get anything back. Then your reward will be great, and you will be sons of the Most High, because he is kind to the ungrateful and wicked.

Treasure Chest

Where's your treasure? I mean where do you put your dough? When I got my first car, every penny I had went into that car. One day my nice new paint job got a scratch from one end of the car to the other. I was so mad. Who would do such a terrible thing? It did more than mess up my week. But in the grand scheme of eternity, that car doesn't get to go with me. It's pointless. When I started dating the girl I married, every penny I had went into gifts for her, dates, dinner. Hey, girls are expensive! But she has my heart. Now I should look at the scripture again and see it as a promise instead of a principle. So here's the question, where do I want my heart? Well I want my heart in the Kingdom of God. So how do I get my heart there? Is it a decision, a song, some sort of ritual I need to perform? Do I just need to picture myself giving my heart to God? Jesus made it clear. He said I need to put my treasure into the Kingdom of God, and that my heart would come along for the ride. Jesus has made His home in my heart, now let me put my heart into His home, His Kingdom. This is what the widow did when she brought just two mites to the temple, a fraction of a penny. Jesus jumped up and said, "Hey, this lady gave more than everyone else!" Why? What did she give? Well, she gave her heart; it was all that she had. Remember, your car ain't going into eternity with you. Now a dude needs a car to get around and do some work, but your car doesn't need your heart, it just needs gas. God wants your heart, and you need that. So pony up some dough. You may be saying, "Oh, all God wants is my money…" No, that's not true. He wants your heart. I want your money. Send your checks and cash to Taking a Minute, P.O. Box, oh, just kidding. Don't send it to me. Send it to the storehouse – your local church.

GOD MAIL: Write down some thoughts you want to share with God.

GOD REPLY: Did you hear any thoughts that you think might be from God? Exercise your ability to hear Him, and write it down here.

GOD LOVE: Who are you praying for today? Become others minded by praying for others needs. God will meet your needs! Help others win and God will help you win.

GOD THOUGHT: What are you choosing to think about today? We should always choose our thoughts!

CONFESSING GOD'S WORD

TEACHING NOTES:

Speaker ____________________

Date ____________________

Topic ____________________

CONFESSING GOD'S WORD:

Say this out loud every day this week!

Matthew 6:21

For where your treasure is, there your heart will be also.

Team Spirit

In Mark 9:38 the disciple John said to Jesus, "We saw a man driving out demons in your name and we told him to stop, because he was not one of us." Well, Jesus reply was, "Don't stop him…" It is interesting that the normal human reaction to Jesus' disciples was to stop this man. The Bible doesn't tell anymore about who this man was, but apparently some other dude had caught the vision of Jesus Christ and was out working it! Jesus is saying, "Hey just because he's not here with us, doesn't mean he's not on the same team." Team Jesus. There are many churches that teach many things, but the unifying factor should be clear: Jesus is the only Son of God who died for our sins, and rose from the dead. Believe in Him and you will be saved. That's Team Jesus. Now there are people who criticize other churches, other leaders, pastors, ministers, take things they say out of context…not recognizing that we are a family, on Team Jesus, searching for truth. Remember that there were twelve different tribes in the nation of Israel, and you may find many different Christian churches, with different vibes in each one. What I'm saying is that there is a lot of division and hate running around among the Christians. It's on the Internet and in the news; people upset with this church, or this view, or that. I've read blogs that make your skin crawl with hate. Let's not be haters, or divisive against those who preach and believe in Christ. Remember that Christ's Word protects us, and if we come against another Christian, we are putting ourselves on the wrong team. Let us bless each other, as God will bless those who bless you. Let us love one another. After all, they will know we are Christians by our love.

GOD MAIL: Write down some thoughts you want to share with God.

GOD REPLY: Did you hear any thoughts that you think might be from God? Exercise your ability to hear Him, and write it down here.

GOD LOVE: Who are you praying for today? Become others minded by praying for others needs. God will meet your needs! Help others win and God will help you win.

GOD THOUGHT: What are you choosing to think about today? We should always choose our thoughts!

CONFESSING GOD'S WORD

TEACHING NOTES:

Speaker ____________________

Date ____________________

Topic ____________________

CONFESSING GOD'S WORD:

Say this out loud every day this week!

Romans 15:5

May the God who gives endurance and encouragement give you a spirit of unity among yourselves as you follow Christ Jesus...

Save the Planet

I want to clear something up. On T.V. the other day I heard a couple of people ask the question, "If there is a God, why is there world hunger?" And I thought to myself, "Isn't it just like mankind to blame God for our problems?" The Israelites were led out of slavery into the desert, and on the journey they became angry. Now God had taken them out of slavery, mind you, and was taking them to a good land, flowing with milk and honey. Well, the people got all mad at Moses and God. I guess things still haven't changed. Well, today, in our world, there are wars, and people are dying, and sometimes people get mad at God about it. But God is love. He sent His Son that we might have life and life more abundantly. It is the devil who comes to steal kill and destroy. One day my 11 year old was all, "Hey, I'm thirsty." And I'm like, "You're 11. Get yourself a drink of water." Look at this. Psalms 115:16 says, "The highest heavens belong to the Lord, but the earth He has given to man." God has asked us to manage this planet, to steward over it, to rule over it, He asked us to take dominion and authority over it. So then, if there is world hunger, we better get to feeding the people. Don't forget we are the hands and feet of Christ. When He wants to get something done He needs us to be obedient. Like when He wanted to part the Red Sea, He told Moses to stretch out his hand over the water. God needed man to obey. So let's be accountable for this world's troubles, and let's get to work on fixing it. Donate some money above your tithes to missions work in your church, volunteer in your local community. Get involved. Get to work. Let's be faithful with this planet, it's our responsibility!!

GOD MAIL: Write down some thoughts you want to share with God.

GOD REPLY: Did you hear any thoughts that you think might be from God? Exercise your ability to hear Him, and write it down here.

GOD LOVE: Who are you praying for today? Become others minded by praying for others needs. God will meet your needs! Help others win and God will help you win.

GOD THOUGHT: What are you choosing to think about today? We should always choose our thoughts!

CONFESSING GOD'S WORD

TEACHING NOTES:

Speaker ________________

Date ________________

Topic ________________

CONFESSING GOD'S WORD:

Say this out loud every day this week!

---

1 Corinthians 3:9

For we are God's fellow workers; you are God's field, God's building.

Whole Wheat or Rye?

Exodus 16:1: "The whole Israelite community set out from Elim and came to the Desert of Sin." Have you ever been to the Desert of Sin? This is the place of temptation in your life. When Jesus taught us to pray, one of the phrases He used was, "Lead us not into temptation." When we arrive in the Desert of Sin in our life, it is probably something we got ourselves into… A place we went, a plan we've made, or a friend that is stringing us along. But, here we are, in the Desert of Sin. How do we keep from falling into the temptations? Well, Jesus starts the prayer by saying, "Give us this day our daily bread." Now He isn't referring to needing toast to start out your day. He's talking about the Word of God. When Jesus was tempted by Satan in the desert he stated plainly, "Man does not live by bread alone, but on every word the proceeds from the mouth of God." So our daily bread is being in the Bible. But how often? Oh yeah, it would be, um, every day. In the Desert of Sin is where God, for the first time, sent the Israelites some food. He rained it down in the morning, and the people called it manna. God referred to it as bread. And He rained it down every day for 40 years so the Israelites would have food. And what God is trying to teach us here is that the world is full of temptation, and the Desert of Sin is located all around – the Internet, the T.V., school, work… but how do you handle it? The strength you need to be victorious every day is hidden in the secrets of God's Word. So get up and make yourself some toast, put some honey on it, and get a glass of milk.

GOD MAIL: Write down some thoughts you want to share with God.

GOD REPLY: Did you hear any thoughts that you think might be from God? Exercise your ability to hear Him, and write it down here.

GOD LOVE: Who are you praying for today? Become others minded by praying for others needs. God will meet your needs! Help others win and God will help you win.

GOD THOUGHT: What are you choosing to think about today? We should always choose our thoughts!

CONFESSING GOD'S WORD

TEACHING NOTES:

Speaker ______________________

Date ______________________

Topic ______________________

CONFESSING GOD'S WORD:

Say this out loud every day this week!

Matthew 4:4

Jesus answered, "It is written: 'Man does not live on bread alone, but on every word that comes from the mouth of God...'"

Say What?

Ruth 3:1: “One day Naomi, Ruth’s mother-in-law, said to her, ‘My daughter, should I not try to find a home for you, where you will be well provided for?’” Ruth’s husband had died, and her mom-in-law here is trying to fix her up with a new guy. Now Ruth has been living it single for a while and seems to be doing fine, but God has a plan for her to hook up with Boaz, who by the way, happens to be in the direct lineage with King David and our Savior, Jesus Christ. So Ruth listens to her mom describe what she can do to make sure Boaz knows she is interested in him. And Ruth says to her mother in law, “I will do whatever you say.” Young people, listen up, part of the key to Ruth’s success was to learn to take some advice from her mom. God did not come down from heaven and speak this to Ruth, this was her mother-in-law. When Jacob needed a wife his mom and dad told him where to go looking. And when Isaac needed a wife, Abraham was the dude who knew where to find his soul mate. So the next time your mom and dad are offering up a hot bowl of what they think you should do, maybe take a spoonful; it may just be what you need to find your path again. Sometimes God will speak to you through them. Have you stopped listening? Does it sometimes just sound like blah blah blah blah. Well let’s translate the blah blah’s. They may just be giving you the keys to your future, and when was the last time you said, like Ruth, “I will do whatever you say.”

GOD MAIL: Write down some thoughts you want to share with God.

GOD REPLY: Did you hear any thoughts that you think might be from God? Exercise your ability to hear Him, and write it down here.

GOD LOVE: Who are you praying for today? Become others minded by praying for others needs. God will meet your needs! Help others win and God will help you win.

GOD THOUGHT: What are you choosing to think about today? We should always choose our thoughts!

CONFESSING GOD'S WORD

TEACHING NOTES:

Speaker ____________________

Date ____________________

Topic ____________________

CONFESSING GOD'S WORD:

Say this out loud every day this week!

Proverbs 12:15

The way of a fool seems right to him, but a wise man listens to advice.

Share and Share Alike

In Matthew 28:5 an angel of the Lord appeared to Mary Magdelene and, um, the other Mary just outside the tomb of where Jesus had been placed after they crucified Him. The angel said to the women, "Do not be afraid, for I know that you are looking for Jesus, who was crucified. He is not here; He has risen, just as He said. Come and see the place where He lay. Then go quickly and tell His disciples." Well so there you go. "Go quickly and tell His disciples" was the instruction. The angel was saying, "Hey, now that you know Jesus is alive, go tell someone. Oh, and make it snappy." He started out by saying, "Do not be afraid." Sharing what we know about Jesus might seem a bit frightening to some people. I mean, what if people think you are a loon? Maybe your good friend will be all, "Leave me alone, you Jesus freak." Or maybe not. Maybe your good friend will be all, "Hey, thanks for helping me." Both outcomes are good because you have been obedient to the Lord. And telling someone may not always produce immediately. Sometimes it's like a seed you plant, that grows over time. But don't be afraid to share your faith. Live a life that is pleasing to God and share Jesus with people around you. They need Him; they need that love and forgiveness just like you. One great and very simple way to do this is to invite someone to church. Remember that God will begin to work on the heart just like He did with you. So go, tell someone, and hurry....

GOD MAIL: Write down some thoughts you want to share with God.

GOD REPLY: Did you hear any thoughts that you think might be from God? Exercise your ability to hear Him, and write it down here.

GOD LOVE: Who are you praying for today? Become others minded by praying for others needs. God will meet your needs! Help others win and God will help you win.

GOD THOUGHT: What are you choosing to think about today? We should always choose our thoughts!

CONFESSING GOD'S WORD

TEACHING NOTES:

Speaker ____________________

Date ____________________

Topic ____________________

CONFESSING GOD'S WORD:

Say this out loud every day this week!

Mark 16:15

He said to them, "Go into all the world and preach the good news to all creation..."

Science or Substance?

Romans 1:20 says, "For since the creation of the world God's invisible qualities—His eternal power and divine nature—have been clearly seen, being understood from what has been made, so that men are without excuse." So by looking at God's amazing creation we can see God's invisible qualities. For instance: In 1919 Edwin Hubble, looking through a telescope, made an enormous discovery. He found that the universe is expanding. He noticed that stars and galaxies are moving away from the earth, and the further away they are, the faster they are moving. The universe is being stretched out, and this is called "Hubble's Law." In The Bible, the book of Isaiah alone refers to the stretching of the heavens four different times. Yeah, Edwin Hubble, God is stretching out the universe. Kind of like when Columbus discovered the earth is round, but the Bible mentioned the Circle of the Earth in Isaiah 40:22 thousands of years before Columbus. And if you've decided to not buy into Darwinian Evolution, and you instead choose to believe in God, then you are joining with the leading physicists of all time who also believe in God, like Sir Isaac Newton, Kepler, Planck, Heisenberg and (drum roll…) Albert Einstein. Einstein, when asked if he believed in Jesus Christ said, "Unquestionably! No one can read the Gospels without feeling the actual presence of Jesus. His personality pulsates in every word. No myth is filled with such life." Yeah, Einstein said that, and well, I agree.

GOD MAIL: Write down some thoughts you want to share with God.

GOD REPLY: Did you hear any thoughts that you think might be from God? Exercise your ability to hear Him, and write it down here.

GOD LOVE: Who are you praying for today? Become others minded by praying for others needs. God will meet your needs! Help others win and God will help you win.

GOD THOUGHT: What are you choosing to think about today? We should always choose our thoughts!

CONFESSING GOD'S WORD

TEACHING NOTES:

Speaker ____________________

Date ____________________

Topic ____________________

CONFESSING GOD'S WORD:

Say this out loud every day this week!

Isaiah 45:18

For this is what the LORD says— he who created the heavens, he is God; he who fashioned and made the earth, he founded it; he did not create it to be empty, but formed it to be inhabited— he says: "I am the LORD, and there is no other..."

An Artist's Portrait

Why is it that people want to get you in trouble? 2000 years ago it was the same. In Matthew 22:19 the Pharisees were trying to get Jesus in trouble, and they asked Jesus, "Is it right to pay taxes to Caesar?" So is it? I mean do you have to pay taxes? What is Jesus' take on taxes? Well Jesus answers a very simple question by adding in the answer to the real questions we are faced with. He gets a coin and says "Whose portrait is on this?" Well they answered him, "It's a portrait of Caesar." Of course in our coins it is Washington or someone like that. So Jesus says "Give to Caesar what is Caesar's." So He's saying it belongs to whose portrait was on it. So, pay your taxes right? Well of course, but then He adds, "and give to God what is God's." Well now here's the answer to the real question. The questions is, who do I belong to? The portrait of God is on you, you were made in His likeness and image. You aren't God, of course, neither is the coin itself Caesar. It is an image of Caesar. You are an image of God, which means you need to give to God what is God's. Jesus wasn't talking about money. He was talking about all of you, everything, to the Lord – your mind, your will, your emotions, your body. Romans 12:1 instructs us to offer our bodies to the Lord. Why? Well, because He needs our hands and feet helping Him make this a better world. Hey, God, here's my mouth, what should I say to my friends? And He's all, "Invite them to meet Me." And so you do.

GOD MAIL: Write down some thoughts you want to share with God.

GOD REPLY: Did you hear any thoughts that you think might be from God? Exercise your ability to hear Him, and write it down here.

GOD LOVE: Who are you praying for today? Become others minded by praying for others needs. God will meet your needs! Help others win and God will help you win.

GOD THOUGHT: What are you choosing to think about today? We should always choose our thoughts!

CONFESSING GOD'S WORD

TEACHING NOTES:

Speaker ________________________

Date ________________________

Topic ________________________

CONFESSING GOD'S WORD:

Say this out loud every day this week!

---

1 Peter 2:9

But you are a chosen people, a royal priesthood, a holy nation, a people belonging to God, that you may declare the praises of him who called you out of darkness into his wonderful light.

A Clean Mess

Acts 7:48 says, "However the most high does not live in houses made by men.. Heaven is my throne and the earth is my footstool, what kind of house will you build for me?" In the first covenant Moses built a tabernacle and then Solomon built a temple for God to live in, but this was not a permanent dwelling. God needed something that wasn't man- made. Well, if it isn't man-made, then it must be something God made. And so He explains in I Corinthians 3:16, "Don't you know that you yourselves are God's temple and that God's Spirit lives in you?" How can God live in man? We are a mess, right? But two important things have taken place that make you the dwelling of the Lord. First, you were created by God. Second, Jesus died and when you choose to believe and receive Christ, your body is washed clean by the blood of Jesus. So God can live in your mess, cause your mess is now clean. Well, this is the New Covenant, and Jesus said in John 15, "Remain in me and I will remain in you." Christ is in us, and we are in Him, so the relationship is: what's His is ours and what's ours is His. We need Him, and God wants us. Why? Well, God put talents and abilities in you to help you change this world, and as you step in to becoming a doer in your life He will give you the supernatural God power to help you win. He's in you. He's your partner, but you are a partner too, so you gotta get out there and start tearing it up for God Yes?

GOD MAIL: Write down some thoughts you want to share with God.

GOD REPLY: Did you hear any thoughts that you think might be from God? Exercise your ability to hear Him, and write it down here.

GOD LOVE: Who are you praying for today? Become others minded by praying for others needs. God will meet your needs! Help others win and God will help you win.

GOD THOUGHT: What are you choosing to think about today? We should always choose our thoughts!

CONFESSING GOD'S WORD

TEACHING NOTES:

Speaker ____________________

Date ____________________

Topic ____________________

CONFESSING GOD'S WORD:

Say this out loud every day this week!

Acts 6:8

Now Stephen, a man full of God's grace and power, did great wonders and miraculous signs among the people.

Rule or Be Ruled

Okay, I get it, gas prices are rising. This makes lots of other prices rise. And the doom and gloom from the news continues. Well I'm the media today, but I've got no doom or gloom for you. God's Word teaches us to focus on the good, not the bad – to speak good, to think positive, to expect the promises of God to be working in us and through us. God's Word shows me that it was during a great famine that Abraham, Isaac, and Joseph became wealthy. We are God's people. Don't let your thoughts or attitude be affected by the reports of famine in your land. The Bible says in Colossians 2:20, "Since you died with Christ to the basic principles of this world, why, as though you still belonged to it, do you submit to its rules?" Now we as Christians are not subject to the circumstances, but we are ruler over the circumstance. When a storm came up on Jesus, He didn't go, "Oh, no! It's rain! I hope we're gonna make it." Instead, He took authority over the circumstance. He has given that same authority to you, but we set ourselves up to lose when we get to thinking about the bad news. Don't let the sadness of the Wall Street Journal be in you, instead, let the joy of the Lord be your strength. When you receive Christ, you enter the Kingdom of God. He has a different set of rules, and oh, umm, streets of gold. So you could just sell some pavement to buy some gas.

GOD MAIL: Write down some thoughts you want to share with God.

GOD REPLY: Did you hear any thoughts that you think might be from God? Exercise your ability to hear Him, and write it down here.

GOD LOVE: Who are you praying for today? Become others minded by praying for others needs. God will meet your needs! Help others win and God will help you win.

GOD THOUGHT: What are you choosing to think about today? We should always choose our thoughts!

CONFESSING GOD'S WORD

TEACHING NOTES:

Speaker ____________________

Date ____________________

Topic ____________________

CONFESSING GOD'S WORD:

Say this out loud every day this week!

1 John 5:4

For everyone born of God overcomes the world. This is the victory that has overcome the world, even our faith.

From Commotion to Promotion

Colossians 3:22 says, "Slaves, obey your earthly masters in everything. And do it with sincerity of heart and reverence for the Lord." Well now, God doesn't want us to be slaves; Jesus came to set the captives free! But He is telling us that we may find ourselves in a position we don't like, being required to do something we don't enjoy. Joseph started out his incredibly successful life as a slave. But Joseph didn't see himself as a slave; he saw himself as someone who works for God. So what is God saying here? In everything we do we should do it as though we are working for the Lord. Joseph worked for God. So we don't have to change what we do, but we are changing why we do it. So whether you find yourself slaving over the stove at In-N-Out Burger, or mopping floors at Wal-Mart, or pitching for the Yankees, or whatever you are doing, make God your reason for doing it. Our God will promote you to new heights. If you can be great doing something you don't enjoy, then you can be great at anything. Now I'm not saying not to strive to find a better position, or to better yourself through education. I am saying that if you make whatever you are doing about God, He will promote you, like Joseph, who went from slave to being second in command of all of Egypt.

GOD MAIL: Write down some thoughts you want to share with God.

GOD REPLY: Did you hear any thoughts that you think might be from God? Exercise your ability to hear Him, and write it down here.

GOD LOVE: Who are you praying for today? Become others minded by praying for others needs. God will meet your needs! Help others win and God will help you win.

GOD THOUGHT: What are you choosing to think about today? We should always choose our thoughts!

CONFESSING GOD'S WORD

TEACHING NOTES:

Speaker ____________________

Date ____________________

Topic ____________________

CONFESSING GOD'S WORD:

Say this out loud every day this week!

Colossians 3:23

Whatever you do, work at it with all your heart, as working for the Lord, not for men...

If You Build It...

Jude 1:20 says, "Build yourselves up in your most holy faith, and pray in the Holy Spirit." Why build yourself up in faith? Well, it is by faith that we receive the promises of God, starting with that first step you took when you decided to receive Christ. That was a step of faith. It was believing in a truth that you had not personally seen for yourself. And it secures for you life forever. Yeah... When Jesus disciples were struggling, He would tell them to have faith in God. Hebrews 11:11 explains that it was by faith that Abraham received his son Isaac that had been promised to him by God. By faith. In Mark 11:24 Jesus says, "Whatever you ask for in prayer, believe that you have received it, and it will be yours." The believing that you have received it, that is faith, believing God that His word is true. So it's not enough just to pray it, we have to believe it! The world says that seeing is believing, but God is saying, "Believe before you see!" Now how do we build ourselves up in faith? Romans 10:17 says, "Faith comes through hearing the message, and the message is heard through the word of Christ." And just above that it says, "And how can they hear without someone preaching to them?" So faith comes by hearing the Word of God preached to us. And where are you going to hear that? Well, duh, that's church.

GOD MAIL: Write down some thoughts you want to share with God.

GOD REPLY: Did you hear any thoughts that you think might be from God? Exercise your ability to hear Him, and write it down here.

GOD LOVE: Who are you praying for today? Become others minded by praying for others needs. God will meet your needs! Help others win and God will help you win.

GOD THOUGHT: What are you choosing to think about today? We should always choose our thoughts!

CONFESSING GOD'S WORD

TEACHING NOTES:

Speaker ____________________

Date ____________________

Topic ____________________

CONFESSING GOD'S WORD:

Say this out loud every day this week!

Hebrews 11:6

And without faith it is impossible to please God, because anyone who comes to him must believe that he exists and that he rewards those who earnestly seek him.

Front and Center

In Luke 20:46 Jesus says, "Beware of the teachers of the law. They like to walk around in flowing robes and love to be greeted in the marketplaces and have the most important seats in the synagogues and the places of honor at banquets." So I guess a modern day interpretation of this might be "Watch out for the people with all the rules. They like to strut around in their really hip clothes, have everyone be all, "Hey, what's up dude?" Now the key word here is that they LOVE those things. Cuz God promises you that He wants to clothe you more splendidly than Solomon, so He's into good clothes. He has prepared a banquet table for you, and when you receive Christ you become royalty. He has made you the head and not the tail. And someone has to sit in the front row at church, so it may as well be you. I mean the kids at school who sat in the front row were always there trying to learn more, and we should be doing that at church. But Jesus said to beware of the people who love these things. We shouldn't care if we have to sit in the back, and we shouldn't think we are all special just cuz we have an expensive suit or dress. Jesus said that the last would be first, and He wants us to serve so that we can lead. Now God still wants to put you in the best seat, with the best duds, but He gets all the glory, cuz what makes you different is Christ.

GOD MAIL: Write down some thoughts you want to share with God.

GOD REPLY: Did you hear any thoughts that you think might be from God? Exercise your ability to hear Him, and write it down here.

GOD LOVE: Who are you praying for today? Become others minded by praying for others needs. God will meet your needs! Help others win and God will help you win.

GOD THOUGHT: What are you choosing to think about today? We should always choose our thoughts!

CONFESSING GOD'S WORD

TEACHING NOTES:

Speaker ______________________________

Date ______________________________

Topic ______________________________

CONFESSING GOD'S WORD:

Say this out loud every day this week!

Deuteronomy 28:13

The LORD will make you the head, not the tail. If you pay attention to the commands of the LORD your God that I give you this day and carefully follow them, you will always be at the top, never at the bottom.

Can I Get That in Hi-Def?

Jesus died for you, and when He died and rose from the dead He accomplished so many things, like redemption from sins, healing, establishing His church, so many things that I couldn't cover them in a minute. But listen to this: Galatians 3:14 says, "He redeemed us in order that the blessing given to Abraham might come to the Gentiles." So according to this, the blessing that God gave Abraham is now available to anyone who receives Christ. So what is that blessing? Genesis 12:2: (now put your name in here) "I will make you into a great nation, and I will bless you; I will make your name great, and you will be a blessing." God is making us into a powerful people, and He wants to make your name great. Why? Because if your name is great, then you have the influence to point others to God. And He will bless you and you will be a blessing. You see, He's not blessing you just so you can have 40 plasma TV's. He wants you to be a blessing! Like King David, who God blessed with great wealth. David gave that wealth to help his son build the temple for God. In I Chronicles 14 it says he gave 3,750 tons of gold to the Lord. That is over 112 billion dollars in gold! Whoa! That's a lot of TVs. David said, "I am seeking wealth for the sake of the House of the Lord." It's never about the money; it's about becoming a blessing to others.

GOD MAIL: Write down some thoughts you want to share with God.

GOD REPLY: Did you hear any thoughts that you think might be from God? Exercise your ability to hear Him, and write it down here.

GOD LOVE: Who are you praying for today? Become others minded by praying for others needs. God will meet your needs! Help others win and God will help you win.

GOD THOUGHT: What are you choosing to think about today? We should always choose our thoughts!

CONFESSING GOD'S WORD

TEACHING NOTES:

Speaker ________________

Date ________________

Topic ________________

CONFESSING GOD'S WORD:

Say this out loud every day this week!

Matthew 6:31-33

So do not worry, saying, 'What shall we eat?' or 'What shall we drink?' or 'What shall we wear?' For the pagans run after all these things, and your heavenly Father knows that you need them. But seek first his kingdom and his righteousness, and all these things will be given to you as well.

You Got Their Back?

So in Genesis 14 four kings are out pillaging and end up picking on Abraham's nephew, who was named Lot. They carried off Lot and all of his possessions, his family, everything. Well, Abraham gets wind of what happened and he sets off to get Lot and his stuff back. He puts together his army, his friends, and heads off to fight against four nations. Verse 14 mentions that Abraham had on his staff 318 trained fighting men. That may have very well been the very first, um, posse. Abraham and his homies. Well they went on to battle and won. Keep in mind that this was not Abraham's problem; no one had attacked him. He was off helping others. Now of course when life gets tough on us, and we feel like we are being attacked, our reaction is to go to battle, ask God for help in prayer. This was different though, Abraham chose to fight for others, to help others. We want to have this same attitude. When someone you know is in distress, call out the trained armies, get your posse, and go and help those who are in need of help. It may seem like it isn't your battle to fight, but like Jesus said, "No greater love has any man than he lay down his life for his friends." As Christians we have a much higher calling than just fighting our own battles. If someone you know is going through a crisis, and it's not your crisis, just watch 'em drown. No, wait! You gotta help. God will help, too.

GOD MAIL: Write down some thoughts you want to share with God.

GOD REPLY: Did you hear any thoughts that you think might be from God? Exercise your ability to hear Him, and write it down here.

GOD LOVE: Who are you praying for today? Become others minded by praying for others needs. God will meet your needs! Help others win and God will help you win.

GOD THOUGHT: What are you choosing to think about today? We should always choose our thoughts!

CONFESSING GOD'S WORD

TEACHING NOTES:

Speaker ______________________

Date ______________________

Topic ______________________

CONFESSING GOD'S WORD:

Say this out loud every day this week!

Luke 3:10-11

"What should we do then?" the crowd asked. John answered, "The man with two tunics should share with him who has none, and the one who has food should do the same."

Your Rep

Remember Daniel, the lions' den guy? Well, through the book of Daniel he is serving under many different foreign kings. These kings were typically ungodly men, worshiping idols of gold and silver and wood and stone, and all around bad dudes. Like working for your Burger Jack burger managers, Daniel served with excellence and found himself often promoted under these kings. And whenever one of these kings had a serious mystery to unveil, a crisis, like when one had a dream that he needed to know the meaning of, or another saw the hand of God writing a message on the wall that no one could read, they would call upon Daniel. Why? Because of his rep. They knew that he knew God. So I guess you could say that when things got critical, they knew who to turn to, the one true God, and the guy who knew him. Okay, so you're Daniel. What does that mean? We are surrounded by people who are living their lives every day not even thinking about the existence of God, but when trouble comes, who are they going to turn to? Be a Daniel in your world, around the people you know. People should know that you have a relationship with God, and that relationship means that you are capable of reading the words of God and understanding what they mean. The Lord speaks to you. Then you can point them to God in their time of need and offer a real answer and mountain moving prayer! It is a gift and an advantage. True wisdom is at your finger tips. Be that person – the one everyone knows knows God.

GOD MAIL: Write down some thoughts you want to share with God.

GOD REPLY: Did you hear any thoughts that you think might be from God? Exercise your ability to hear Him, and write it down here.

GOD LOVE: Who are you praying for today? Become others minded by praying for others needs. God will meet your needs! Help others win and God will help you win.

GOD THOUGHT: What are you choosing to think about today? We should always choose our thoughts!

CONFESSING GOD'S WORD

TEACHING NOTES:

Speaker __________

Date __________

Topic __________

CONFESSING GOD'S WORD:

Say this out loud every day this week!

Matthew 5:14

You are the light of the world. A city on a hill cannot be hidden.

God Seekers

Matthew 9: Jesus went through all the towns and villages teaching in the synagogues. Where did He teach? The synagogues. Well that's like church. Mark 1:39 says, "So he traveled throughout Galilee, preaching in their synagogues…" Luke 4: "And Jesus went into the synagogue…" Sounds like Jesus spent a bunch of time teaching and preaching at the churches in each city. As the Bible is telling the story of Christ four different times, each finds him travelling around and stopping to teach in the church. This is a picture for us to follow, that the Word of God is drawn to the church, and should flow from the church. Remember that Jesus is the Word. When people run out of their own ideas and finally decide to seek God, where do they find themselves? I was watching a movie the other day, and the character hit rock bottom and found himself where? Walking into a downtown church, down the aisle and falling on his face. Church continues to be a symbol of hope, offering sanctuary to those who seek the Lord. Jesus knew His target market. His target was those who were seeking God. He said it this way: "Seek and you will find". People find God when they are seeking Him. So get on out there and bring the lost into the church. Invite the hurting to come and find healing in the Word of God. Get plugged into your church, and help build it! Grab a flyer from the church and hand it out. Hang up posters. Bring the world to the church, where the Word of God is flowing!

GOD MAIL: Write down some thoughts you want to share with God.

GOD REPLY: Did you hear any thoughts that you think might be from God? Exercise your ability to hear Him, and write it down here.

GOD LOVE: Who are you praying for today? Become others minded by praying for others needs. God will meet your needs! Help others win and God will help you win.

GOD THOUGHT: What are you choosing to think about today? We should always choose our thoughts!

CONFESSING GOD'S WORD

TEACHING NOTES:

Speaker ____________________

Date ____________________

Topic ____________________

CONFESSING GOD'S WORD:

Say this out loud every day this week!

Habakkak 2:14

For the earth will be filled with the knowledge of the glory of the LORD, as the waters cover the sea.

Whoa, Look at You

How nice is your car? Mine is really nice. Whoa, is that okay? I John 3:17 says, "If anyone has material possessions and sees his brother in need but has no pity on him, how can the love of God be in him?" Remember the goal? Love. God is love and He is drawing us closer to Him. Imitate God, right? It's funny how sometimes we can have plenty, but we look at someone who has even more and we think we have nothing. Comparing with others can really mess you up. The question is: Do you have more than you need? God will bless you with what the Bible refers to as more than you can contain. The reason it is more than you can contain is because you need to give the overflow away; it is for others in need. Again, He said "If anyone has material possessions…" You see having put you in a position to give, which helps you show that the Love of God is in you. David was a very wealthy man, and was considered a man after God's heart. God wants you to be blessed so that you can give, showing His love. The promises of God are there for us that we might become a blessing. It should not lead to greed or buying a bunch of stuff you don't need, stuff you can't take with you, stuff that rots. Instead be a blessing, store up treasures in heaven, let the love of God within you shine. And as you give, it will be given back to you, pressed down, shaken together, and running over. Then you have even more that you have to try and give away.

GOD MAIL: Write down some thoughts you want to share with God.

GOD REPLY: Did you hear any thoughts that you think might be from God? Exercise your ability to hear Him, and write it down here.

GOD LOVE: Who are you praying for today? Become others minded by praying for others needs. God will meet your needs! Help others win and God will help you win.

GOD THOUGHT: What are you choosing to think about today? We should always choose our thoughts!

CONFESSING GOD'S WORD

TEACHING NOTES:

Speaker ____________________

Date ____________________

Topic ____________________

CONFESSING GOD'S WORD:

Say this out loud every day this week!

Luke 6:38

Give, and it will be given to you. A good measure, pressed down, shaken together and running over, will be poured into your lap. For with the measure you use, it will be measured to you."

Does Your Toilet Shine?

When I was in high school I worked at Dunkin' Donuts. (Hey, don't mock it – free donuts!) Anyway, one of my jobs was cleaning the bathroom. That was a dirty job. The first time I cleaned the bathroom I really got in there and scrubbed it down, got her shiny and smelling good. But every day it would get messy again. After awhile it made me want to not clean it. K, can people remember to flush? I was getting tired of doing a good job. Galatians 6:9 says, "Let us not become weary in doing good, for at the proper time we will reap a harvest if we do not give up." Anyone can do average work, or get tired of pushing themselves. Most do. God wants us to excel in everything we do, and here He is telling us that if we will stay at it, not getting tired, but push to do well at everything we do, including how we live our lives and the choices we make, we will find ourselves beginning to excel. Most people will give up after a time, but the one who does not give up, instead he endures, pushing to be great at the most mundane and unglamorous of tasks, or cleaning up the bathroom in our lives, the one who presses on and through will reap the harvest in the end. And a harvest that comes from God is going to be more reward than you could've imagined. So no giving up – go get the Pine-Sol!

GOD MAIL: Write down some thoughts you want to share with God.

GOD REPLY: Did you hear any thoughts that you think might be from God? Exercise your ability to hear Him, and write it down here.

GOD LOVE: Who are you praying for today? Become others minded by praying for others needs. God will meet your needs! Help others win and God will help you win.

GOD THOUGHT: What are you choosing to think about today? We should always choose our thoughts!

CONFESSING GOD'S WORD

TEACHING NOTES:

Speaker __________

Date __________

Topic __________

CONFESSING GOD'S WORD:

Say this out loud every day this week!

1 Timothy 4:15

Be diligent in these matters; give yourself wholly to them, so that everyone may see your progress.

Flogging Free Zone

In Acts 22 Paul, the servant of God who wrote much of the New Testament inspired by the Holy Spirit, was taken prisoner. They were flogging him, which is not a word we use much anymore, but it can't be a good thing, and in verse 25 Paul says, "Is it legal for you to flog a Roman Citizen who hasn't even been found guilty?" Well, at this the guard and commanders stopped and got worried. You see, a Roman citizen had great protection. Not because of any reason except for where he was born. It wasn't anything Paul had earned. This is a picture for you and me, because when you receive Christ, you are born into a new Kingdom, that is the Kingdom of God. You are a son of God, brother of Christ, sharing the inheritance of Christ and His glory. You are a citizen of the Kingdom of God who has special protections and privileges. Paul was being flogged. But the story began to change when he let them know he was a citizen of Rome. When this world deals you a losing hand, or you feel like life is "flogging" you, remind yourself and this world that you are a citizen of the Kingdom of God. God who created the heavens and the earth is your Father. And it's not because of what you have done, it is because of where you are born, born into God's kingdom through your faith in Jesus Christ! Galatians 3:26: "You are all sons of God through faith in Christ Jesus." So no flogging for you. Not any more.

GOD MAIL: Write down some thoughts you want to share with God.

GOD REPLY: Did you hear any thoughts that you think might be from God? Exercise your ability to hear Him, and write it down here.

GOD LOVE: Who are you praying for today? Become others minded by praying for others needs. God will meet your needs! Help others win and God will help you win.

GOD THOUGHT: What are you choosing to think about today? We should always choose our thoughts!

CONFESSING GOD'S WORD

TEACHING NOTES:

Speaker ____________________

Date ____________________

Topic ____________________

CONFESSING GOD'S WORD:

Say this out loud every day this week!

Isaiah 43:1

But now, this is what the LORD says— he who created you, O Jacob, he who formed you, O Israel: "Fear not, for I have redeemed you; I have summoned you by name; you are mine.

Bread Check

At my daughter's birthday party there must have been like 30 people at my house. Feeding them, yikes, that's a lot of food. In John 6 a huge crowd had gathered to see Jesus at dinner time, 5000 men and then some women and children. Now these people had apparently not planned ahead for dinner, no picnic baskets or sandwiches, so Jesus sets out to feed them all. The only one who brought some food was a boy. Well Jesus prays over the 5 loaves of bread and 2 fish that the boy brought, and the food went out and fed everyone and there was food left over. First we should note that these were not starving refugees or something. There is nothing to indicate that these people were in some sort of famine, a dire need to eat. They simply had not brought any food. Also, skipping a meal would not have been crazy to do. Most of us could stand to skip a meal. I mean they came without food, so why is it so important that Jesus fed them? Well, this was a picture of how Jesus wishes to feed all of us, not barley and fish, but the Word of God. It's supernatural food that is more important to our lives and happiness than regular food, but are we eating? Man lives on every word that proceeds from the mouth of God. Maybe you didn't plan on eating some Word today, but Jesus is praying and multiplying it for you anyways. Grab yourself a Bible, or a podcast, and get some bread in you every day. The Word is what changes and grows us. The Bible has the wisdom you need for everything you're facing now or will ever face.

GOD MAIL: Write down some thoughts you want to share with God.

GOD REPLY: Did you hear any thoughts that you think might be from God? Exercise your ability to hear Him, and write it down here.

GOD LOVE: Who are you praying for today? Become others minded by praying for others needs. God will meet your needs! Help others win and God will help you win.

GOD THOUGHT: What are you choosing to think about today? We should always choose our thoughts!

CONFESSING GOD'S WORD

TEACHING NOTES:

Speaker ____________________

Date ____________________

Topic ____________________

CONFESSING GOD'S WORD:

Say this out loud every day this week!

Psalms 119:37

Turn my eyes away from worthless things; preserve my life according to your word.

Think, Think, Think

Have you ever lost something, you're all looking for it, then someone says, "Well, where did you set it down?" Colossians 3:1: "Since then you have been raised with Christ, set your hearts on things above." Then it goes on to say, "Set your minds on things above." Where do you set your heart? "Well, I really had my heart set on a piece of that cheesecake." Or maybe you set your heart on some boy. How about your mind, what is your mind set on? Your mind gets set on whatever you spend your time thinking the most, or what you are watching or listening to and surrounding yourself with, and your heart will follow closely behind. Thoughts are seeds that plant in your heart. If you are thinking about God's Word, you plant seeds in your heart that grow up into love, wisdom, joy and peace. If you are thinking about ice cream you will grow in your heart the very strong urge to eat some ice cream. It's your decision where to set your heart and mind. It should be on things above, things of God, like helping our friends be successful, praying, reading the Word of God, finding a way to get along with our brother, or honor our parents, giving, being a great wife or husband, or parent, or kid. Some might say, "Well, those aren't normal things to think about." Yeah, I know, but God doesn't want you to just be normal; He has made you extraordinary!

GOD MAIL: Write down some thoughts you want to share with God.

GOD REPLY: Did you hear any thoughts that you think might be from God? Exercise your ability to hear Him, and write it down here.

GOD LOVE: Who are you praying for today? Become others minded by praying for others needs. God will meet your needs! Help others win and God will help you win.

GOD THOUGHT: What are you choosing to think about today? We should always choose our thoughts!

CONFESSING GOD'S WORD

TEACHING NOTES:

Speaker ____________________

Date ____________________

Topic ____________________

CONFESSING GOD'S WORD:

Say this out loud every day this week!

Phillipians 4:8

Finally, brothers, whatever is true, whatever is noble, whatever is right, whatever is pure, whatever is lovely, whatever is admirable—if anything is excellent or praiseworthy—think about such things.

Joy – A New Energy Drink

I remember working out in high school, and to really push myself I would imagine myself getting all angry about something. I thought anger made me stronger. People talk about all sorts of stuff that makes them stronger, but usually it's something negative. Nehemiah 8:10 says, "For the joy of the Lord is your strength." God's idea of where your strength should come from is much different. Oh, and remember this, God is always right. He says it should come from His joy. Well it's not always easy to be happy, but this lesson is about learning to change your attitude. Joy isn't something you get from having lots of stuff, or having a perfect day. Joy must come first. Even Jesus for the joy set before Him endured the cross. Joy was His strength that day, the day He was crucified, so that He would win. The joy comes before the perfect day, not after. And if you can change your attitude to always being positive and happy, who do you benefit? Well, yourself. If you choose to have a bad attitude, you are ruining your own day. You choose every day how happy you will be, which means you choose how much you will enjoy this life. And the level of joy you choose will determine how strong you will become at overcoming the things of this world. Remember one thing that is easy for you to change is how you feel. And you can feel happy.

GOD MAIL: Write down some thoughts you want to share with God.

GOD REPLY: Did you hear any thoughts that you think might be from God? Exercise your ability to hear Him, and write it down here.

GOD LOVE: Who are you praying for today? Become others minded by praying for others needs. God will meet your needs! Help others win and God will help you win.

GOD THOUGHT: What are you choosing to think about today? We should always choose our thoughts!

CONFESSING GOD'S WORD

TEACHING NOTES:

Speaker ________________________

Date ________________________

Topic ________________________

CONFESSING GOD'S WORD:

Say this out loud every day this week!

Psalms 28:7

The LORD is my strength and my shield; my heart trusts in him, and I am helped. My heart leaps for joy and I will give thanks to him in song.

It Ain't Over 'Til It's Over

Who's attacking you today? In Isaiah 54:15 God says to us, "If anyone does attack you, it will not be My doing; whoever attacks you will surrender to you." This scripture is referring to the covenant that God has made to us through Jesus Christ. The covenant is a new one. God is the same, but the relationship has changed. Your relationship with God is different than the relationship the people had with God before Jesus came and died for us. It is said in Hebrews to be a "new and better covenant." According to the first scripture here, there will still be some battles to face. Rats, I thought it would just be all smooth sailing now. Many people think that being a Christian means you never get attacked. But here you can plainly see that attacks will still come. It's a crazy world and we have a real enemy. Paul was imprisoned and shipwrecked, the Israelites rebelled against Moses, and Batman was attacked by Raz Agul. The key is the promise that God gives: whoever attacks you will surrender to you. So even in the middle of your messy circumstances, remember that you already know the outcome. God is not the attacker. He is not the problem! God is the solution to your problems, and He has promised the solution for you is victory. That is… that they surrender to you.

GOD MAIL: Write down some thoughts you want to share with God.

GOD REPLY: Did you hear any thoughts that you think might be from God? Exercise your ability to hear Him, and write it down here.

GOD LOVE: Who are you praying for today? Become others minded by praying for others needs. God will meet your needs! Help others win and God will help you win.

GOD THOUGHT: What are you choosing to think about today? We should always choose our thoughts!

CONFESSING GOD'S WORD

TEACHING NOTES:

Speaker ______________________

Date ______________________

Topic ______________________

CONFESSING GOD'S WORD:

Say this out loud every day this week!

John 16:33

"I have told you these things, so that in me you may have peace. In this world you will have trouble. But take heart! I have overcome the world."

Yeah, Yeah, Patience. How Long Will That Take?

The motor vehicle department… just a quick stop to get something is going to be a very long wait, so we all avoid it. I was at a stop light today, and I wasn't looking up when the light turned green and there was a quick blast of horns honking behind me. We are not the most patient of people. Ordering fast food, and anymore than like 3 minutes and we are getting angry. Or maybe it's just me. Hebrews 6:12 says, "We do not want you to become lazy, but to imitate those who through faith and patience inherit what has been promised." God wants us to inherit the promises, a land flowing with milk and honey, but these come by faith and patience. Faith is: I am asking God in prayer, and believing that I have received what I ask for in the name of Jesus. But then how many times are we all, "Well I prayed and nothing happened." Yeah, it's only been like 3 minutes. God's not the fry cook in the back banging out burgers at your beck and call. He's resting, and His Word is working now. The promises are available to us, but, my friend, be patient. Don't get discouraged and give up. Abraham waited over 25 years before his promised son Isaac was born. When we get discouraged and give up in our faith, we are described as being lazy. Anyone can give up. That's the easy way out. But that's not you, so order up a burger and fries, it's coming down the pike, but not always as quickly as you might hope.

GOD MAIL: Write down some thoughts you want to share with God.

GOD REPLY: Did you hear any thoughts that you think might be from God? Exercise your ability to hear Him, and write it down here.

GOD LOVE: Who are you praying for today? Become others minded by praying for others needs. God will meet your needs! Help others win and God will help you win.

GOD THOUGHT: What are you choosing to think about today? We should always choose our thoughts!

CONFESSING GOD'S WORD

TEACHING NOTES:

Speaker ____________________

Date ____________________

Topic ____________________

CONFESSING GOD'S WORD:

Say this out loud every day this week!

James 1:3-4

Because you know that the testing of your faith develops perseverance. Perseverance must finish its work so that you may be mature and complete, not lacking anything.

Shut the Door!

My brother and I battled a lot growing up. He's older, so I think he did most of beating, and I did most of the taking it. I survived though, and we are best friends now. Looking back, we both wish we hadn't fought over such small things. I'm over it now. But he did pick on me a lot. But I'm over it… hmmm. Anyways, Cain and Abel fought too. Cain was angry with Abel and the Lord spoke to Cain in Genesis 4:6: "Sin is crouching at your door, it desires to have you, but you must master it." Sin is the wrong decision he was thinking of making cuz he was really mad. Sin desires to have you. It's what it does, and if it can have you, it can destroy you. Like the kid who takes drugs once and ends up with Hepatitis C from a needle, or Aids, or the drunk kid who kills someone driving, or the moment of passion that leaves you empty and cold. It wants to destroy you. It's crouching at your door when you start entertaining it in your mind, thinking about these things, and hanging out with the wrong crowd in the wrong places. God is telling us we are to master sin, to be in control. Sin is your responsibility to stop. Jesus has defeated its power over you, but you must still choose not to open that door and let it leap inside and make a mess. Cain opened the door and let the enemy, the destroyer, right into his life. But you can learn from Cain's mistake. Be bigger than that. Identify the enemy, sin, and keep that door shut!!

GOD MAIL: Write down some thoughts you want to share with God.

GOD REPLY: Did you hear any thoughts that you think might be from God? Exercise your ability to hear Him, and write it down here.

GOD LOVE: Who are you praying for today? Become others minded by praying for others needs. God will meet your needs! Help others win and God will help you win.

GOD THOUGHT: What are you choosing to think about today? We should always choose our thoughts!

CONFESSING GOD'S WORD

TEACHING NOTES:

Speaker ____________________

Date ____________________

Topic ____________________

CONFESSING GOD'S WORD:

Say this out loud every day this week!

James 4:7

Submit yourselves, then, to God. Resist the devil, and he will flee from you.

The 'Rents

Well the 10 Commandments aren't around as much as they used to be and aren't quite "in style" right now socially. But I think they are making a comeback. They are the principles of God for a good life, like don't worship other gods (like your money), take a day off to relax with your family and focus on God (Sabbath), don't kill, don't steal, don't lie about your neighbor, oh, and here's one I want to talk about today... Honor your mother and father. Now this is a command with a promise, "that it may go well with you and you may live a long life." Now you probably like the idea of things going well with you, and long life is better than short life. The command does not have an exception clause, like honor your mother and father unless they aren't perfect people. Maybe you think they don't deserve honor. Maybe one of 'em left you, or both, or maybe you never felt loved. To the world these are all good reasons to not honor them, but God wants you to honor them anyway. Love your parents if for no other reason than they are a big part of why you are alive. Love them unconditionally, not because they earned it. Their actions do not determine your need to be obedient to God. So find things to be thankful for, speak positively about them, give to them, again, not because they are perfect, but because God asks you to. Sow this honor and you will reap honor, and a good long life. It's a promise!

GOD MAIL: Write down some thoughts you want to share with God.

GOD REPLY: Did you hear any thoughts that you think might be from God? Exercise your ability to hear Him, and write it down here.

GOD LOVE: Who are you praying for today? Become others minded by praying for others needs. God will meet your needs! Help others win and God will help you win.

GOD THOUGHT: What are you choosing to think about today? We should always choose our thoughts!

CONFESSING GOD'S WORD

TEACHING NOTES:

Speaker ______________________

Date ______________________

Topic ______________________

CONFESSING GOD'S WORD:

Say this out loud every day this week!

John 13:34

A new command I give you: Love one another. As I have loved you, so you must love one another.

Does God Have a Christmas Wish List?

Hey it's Christmas time. Oops, I said Christmas. Although the trend is to make it about the season's greetings or some other thing, remember that the entire world is either celebrating or at least impacted by the day that represents Jesus birth. And although theologians argue about which day He was actually born, this is the day we celebrate, and so we can celebrate it all the more. Christ gave all to us, His whole life for us. That is why we are reminded to imitate Christ at this time, to give to each other. We should be giving all year round, but since Christmas time is a great reminder for that, let's think about the kind of gifts that mean the most. Like the family less fortunate who could use even an extra $50 to help them, or some Christmas food, or giving a hug. A hug can mean more to your family than an expensive gift. How about the time you spend with others? Time is more valuable than money. How about really writing your feelings in a card that you give? Gifts fade, but memories have the ability to last a lifetime. An encouraging word can change someone's value of themselves – what a wonderful gift to give. Do things that bring unity – in your church, in your family, everywhere. Give financially to your church so that more people can hear the Word of God and be touched. Then they can reach out to more ministries. I mean who better to give to during Christmas than to give a gift to Jesus as a small token of our gratitude, so that the gift of Jesus can continue to be spread. Let's think about the real gifts this year. Oh, and how about this, Merry Jesus Christ's Birthday! Ha!

GOD MAIL: Write down some thoughts you want to share with God.

GOD REPLY: Did you hear any thoughts that you think might be from God? Exercise your ability to hear Him, and write it down here.

GOD LOVE: Who are you praying for today? Become others minded by praying for others needs. God will meet your needs! Help others win and God will help you win.

GOD THOUGHT: What are you choosing to think about today? We should always choose our thoughts!

CONFESSING GOD'S WORD

TEACHING NOTES:

Speaker ____________________

Date ____________________

Topic ____________________

CONFESSING GOD'S WORD:

Say this out loud every day this week!

Proverbs 11:25

A generous man will prosper; he who refreshes others will himself be refreshed.

Upgrade

Another New Year? Really? Oh, and look at you, went a little crazy with the Christmas cookies this year, eh? What does a new year bring to us? God created the seasons, the days, the weeks, these different periods of time that we as humans mirror. A new day is a new beginning, like rebooting your computer. And every year is like a brand new computer, a chance to start something. What is that for you? Do you need some new software? How about some upgrades? I know I could use some more memory. God has infinitely more in mind for you. He is a God without limits. His Word holds this entire universe together. Now, He tells us in James 1:5, "If any of you lacks wisdom, he should ask God who gives generously to all without finding fault." Sometimes we think God isn't going to give us something because of our faults. But our gifts are not earned, they are… well gifts. Wisdom is the ultimate upgrade. We made some mistakes last year, and we need to let the past be in the past, and press on to the future. Wisdom is the ability to step over mistakes, to see problems coming and have a godly solution for whatever is thrown your way. Wisdom will keep us out of mistakes this year. So stop what you are doing and ask the Lord for wisdom. Now, believe that He is giving it to you, do not doubt. Voila!, More memory. Now, uhh, what was I talking about?

GOD MAIL: Write down some thoughts you want to share with God.

GOD REPLY: Did you hear any thoughts that you think might be from God? Exercise your ability to hear Him, and write it down here.

GOD LOVE: Who are you praying for today? Become others minded by praying for others needs. God will meet your needs! Help others win and God will help you win.

GOD THOUGHT: What are you choosing to think about today? We should always choose our thoughts!

CONFESSING GOD'S WORD

TEACHING NOTES:

Speaker ____________________

Date ____________________

Topic ____________________

CONFESSING GOD'S WORD:

Say this out loud every day this week!

Isaiah 43:19

Behold, I am doing a new thing! Now it springs forth; do you not perceive and know it and will you not give heed to it? I will even make a way in the wilderness and rivers in the desert.

Salvation Prayer

Salvation does not mean following a bunch of rules to try and keep God happy. The truth is that He loves you and wants you to experience joy, health, peace and prosperity. You can only do that by knowing Jesus as a friend and savior.

How can you be saved? It is a matter of simply believing.

The Bible says:
If you confess with your mouth the Lord Jesus and believe in your heart that God has raised Him from the dead, you will be saved. ***-Romans 10:9***

If you believe, then pray this prayer:
"Dear Father God I ask you to forgive me of all of my sins. Jesus, come into my heart, come in to my life, be my Lord and Savior. In Jesus name, Amen. Jesus is Lord!"

Congratulations! You have made the very best decision you have ever made or ever will make. Now you are saved. You are forgiven and you are on your way to heaven. The next step is to grow in this new relationship with God. The best way to do that is to read your Bible every day so that God can speak to you through it and get involved in a good church so that you can have support and fellowship of other believers.

Now that you are saved, we would love to hear from you!
Please call us at (480) 964-4463 so that we can come into agreement with you and bless you with a free Bible.

CONTACT US

To order products or for more information contact us at:

Living Word Bible Church
3520 East Brown Road
Mesa, Arizona 85213
Phone: (480) 964-4463

or visit our website at: livingwordonline.org.

TELEVISION BROADCASTS

Join the Anderson's television broadcasts which can be seen in the United States and around the world on stations such as, TBN, Day Star, Fox, TCC, UPN, AZTV and WBUW. Check your local listings for times and stations in your area.

Becoming a partner with Winners' Team helps us extends our outreach to the entire world. As a partner you help us influence the world in four major areas; Crisis Response, Evangelism, Television and Media, and Helping those in Need.

We are one of the only foundations in the world where every single dollar you give goes directly to help others. Because of our partnerships we do not need to use any donations for indirect costs such as office space, overhead, utilities, or other indirect expenses. Give with confidence that all funds are forwarded towards our four major outreaches.

WTP currently has orphanages in India, supports Destiny Orphanage in Uganda, and Hope Unlimited of Brazil. Recently we have engaged in building homes for families in Cambodia who are experiencing a need we can hardly comprehend. We sent a team to preach the gospel in Cambodia, and they visited this sight to survey the need. We are setting out to build 1,000 homes in this community. For every one time donation of $2,500, we will send you a photo of the family and house you helped build over the next three years, in addition your families name will be stamped into the foundation of that home.

You can personally help the ministry efforts of the Winners' Team Partners by joining the team, and becoming a partner in aiding these people. To find extensive information about the nations we are reaching, join the team by calling us at 480-964-4463 or visit us on the web at www.winnersteampartners.com.